The Amazing Mazie Baker

Caitlin Press Inc.
8100 Alderwood Road,
Halfmoon Bay, BC V0N 1Y1
www.caitlin-press.com

Edited by Betty Keller
Text and cover design by Vici Johnstone
Cover image Wendy Lockhart
Printed in Canada

Caitlin Press Inc. acknowledges the Government of Canada, the Canada Council for the Arts, and the British Columbia Arts Council for their financial support for our publishing program.

Library and Archives Canada Cataloguing in Publication
Johnston, Kay, 1941-, author
        The amazing Mazie Baker : the story of a Squamish Nation's warrior elder
/ Kay Johnston.

Includes bibliographical references and index.
ISBN 978-1-987915-06-8 (paperback)
        1. Baker, Mazie. 2. Squamish Indians—Biography. 3. Indian women—Canada—Biography. 4. Native activists—Canada—Biography. I. Title.

E99.S7J65 2016   971.004'9794   C2016-
903668-5

The Amazing Mazie Baker

THE SQUAMISH NATION'S WARRIOR ELDER

Kay Johnston

CAITLIN PRESS

Mazie's dedication

This is my legacy to all my children, my grandchildren and great grandchildren. I am so proud and love you all.

I also dedicate it to all the Native women who are still fighting for their rights. Stay strong and keep fighting.

It is my hope that if other women know that someone like me could stand up and fight, it might even help them to stand up for what they believe in or want.

Kay's dedication

I raise my hands to honour Mazie for sharing her life, family, passion, wisdom and humour, and to Wendy, a warrior in her own right, for sharing her vast knowledge, her strength, courage and spirit.

Foreword

Mazie Baker was an unusual woman.

In working with her and Wendy on the rights of Aboriginal women I learned how women of her generation had been tutored by their aboriginal culture that they did not need "rights" as mainstream society defines them because they had been led to believe that the chiefs and council would look after them. When Mazie learned this was not the case, it empowered her to work with her niece to change the system.

A hard and lonely fight! And a learning experience for me as a politician.

— Senator Pat Carney

INTRODUCTION

S quamish Nation elder Mazie Baker was a formidable fighter for her family and her people and for Native women's rights, despite the fact that she was illiterate. As a member of the post-residential school "lost generation," she grew up without benefit of a direct knowledge of her culture or language, yet somehow through the strict upbringing provided by her parents, she absorbed the values of respect for family, the people and the land. These values became woven into every stage of her life.

I met Mazie in August 1999 while writing *Spirit of Powwow* with her daughter, Gloria Nahanee, organizer of the Squamish Nation Powwow. I was taking photos to illustrate the book when I wandered over to the longhouse on the Capilano Reserve where food was being sold. As no powwow is complete without bannock or Indian bread, I joined the very long lineup. Finally it was my turn and I had a piece of fresh, warm bannock in my hand. It had definitely been worth the wait. When I caught up with Gloria later and told her the bannock was wonderful, she smiled and said, "My mom makes it. Go over to her house and get a picture of her making it for the book." I arrived to find this tiny woman in her kitchen looking like a ghost: her clothes, hands, face and hair were all dusted with flour. She was surrounded by frying pans, mixing bowls, bags of flour, boxes and piles of fresh bannock, and the place was humming as she and two helpers ran an assembly line with a driver waiting for all the boxes to be filled to make the next "bannock run" to the powwow. To my amazement thousands of pieces of bannock were made in that tiny kitchen over the three days of the powwow.

I learned that Mazie was well known on the Mission Reserve in North Vancouver for making political waves while fighting for better communication between chiefs and band councillors and band members, whom she always referred to as "her people." Some of these battles were very bitter, and she had won many — though not all. When her husband died in 1993, the bottom had fallen out of her world, but his death became the catalyst for a life-changing decision: she would plunge more deeply into politics, especially Native women's rights. Her family feared for her safety because she was so outspoken and had already made powerful enemies, but she was undeterred. She set out to learn the language of politics, sharpened her focus and began spending her days planning strategies, talking to groups and committees, and familiarizing herself with all kinds of government documents, a difficult task for someone who could not read. However, she was joined in her crusades by her niece, Wendy Lockhart, and together they became a formidable team.

When they began their fight for Native women's rights, they worked more or less on their own, but as they became aware that there were other women, just like them, across the country fighting the same fight, they began travelling to speak at political meetings and other gatherings, and gradually became recognized as women of power. Soon the Squamish Nation's governance and land policies became fuel for major political confrontations, and there were long drawn-out battles at both the band and federal level. Ultimately, with massive support from the people, they orchestrated the defeat of their chiefs and councillors' plans for self-government, causing ripples of shock across the country.

As I got to know Mazie, I discovered she was highly opinionated and knew no fear when fighting for what she believed to be fair for her people and her family. And the more I discovered about her accomplishments the more I asked myself how she had managed to achieve so much. I became passionate about her story and knew it needed to be told, but would she agree? In June 2007 I asked if she would be interested in working with me to write her story. She was obviously surprised, but I couldn't tell if she liked the idea or not. Finally she said, "Well, I'll think about it, okay?" Well, I thought, she didn't say no.

A few days later she phoned to ask me to drop by. She wanted to talk to me about "this book." I was nervous as we sat chatting about everything but the book until she shifted in her chair and picked up a photo of herself on the steps of the Houses of Parliament. I waited. Then she said:

> Every time I look at this photo of me, Mazie Baker, who can't read or write, standing on the steps of the Houses of Parliament in Ottawa, just before I'm going to speak to a Senate Committee on behalf of my people, I shake my head and wonder, how on earth did all this happen? I look back now at the path I travelled to get there and realize it was really long and tough on me and my family. I had to learn so much and fight so often for the same things over and over. I know deep inside that I was somehow prepared for this by my mom and dad from the time when I was just a little kid. They were both proud and strong and they brought us up to be proud too. They were very strict with us though. I was the youngest and a handful — so I've been told.

I was still sitting on the edge of my seat. Was she going to say yes or no? Meanwhile, Mazie continued chatting, seemingly unaware of my tension. (Later she admitted with a twinkle in her eyes that she knew and was just teasing me.)

She said, "I tell everyone now that was when my journey started. It makes a really good excuse for all the trouble I managed to get into." She eased around in her chair, lifted her bottle of water, laughed and said:

> I haven't changed much, though maybe I'm better at it now after all my years of practice. But it was so much fun! 'Course, I never imagined I would be asked if I was willing to have my life's story written down. At first I was sort of nervous about it. Who would want to read about all the fights I had with the band council to get fair treatment for our people? Would anyone be interested in how my kids helped revive the old ways even though their mother never knew nothing about the language or the culture? Maybe all that political stuff I had to learn would bore them silly. But the ideas and memories kept popping up in my head at the strangest times, and I

started having fun with this. Maybe my story could be a kind of legacy for my kids. If other women could know that someone like me could stand up and fight, it might even help them to stand up for what they believe in or what they want. So I decided it would be good thing for me to do — but I have rules: this is my story, my memories as I remember them, right or wrong.

Then laughing, Mazie added, "Mind you, I'm always right." Then she looked me in the eye and asked, "You ready?"

I had my answer. "Let's get started," I said.

Tape recording was the obvious answer for our collaboration, and Mazie wanted a small one she could carry around and use anytime. She called the taping her homework. "Here I am in my seventies doing homework — Ha!" Over the next five years we became close friends as we worked at her dining table, surrounded by the dozens of family photos and memorabilia that covered the walls and sat on every shelf. On a good day we would fill a whole tape, but we were often interrupted by people dropping in to chat, to ask for advice or help, and we would have to hit "pause" and wait until it was quiet again. She was a joy to work with, always eloquent, with a sizzling sense of humour and scathing opinions.

As you read this book and share Mazie Baker's life, you may not agree with everything she said or believed, but you will be impressed by what she achieved.

1

Mazie Baker based her life on the traditional values of the Squamish people's matriarchal society: respect had to be earned; chiefs must listen to and care for the people; the land, its plants and animals were gifts from the Creator and as such were precious; and spiritualism and ceremony were crucial to the proper functioning of this ancient system of government. These values were woven throughout every stage of her adult life, sometimes at great cost to herself.

Yet Mazie, a member of the post-residential school generation, had not grown up in this kind of society. As a child, she never experienced the old ceremonies or heard the stories of her people's history and legends. She did not even understand her people's language. She knew nothing of their culture. By the time she came into the world, the Indian Act of 1876 had successfully replaced the traditional society of her people with a male-dominated, non-spiritual, capitalistic society. She would spend most of her life fighting to move her people back to their roots.

Mazie was born in St. Paul's Hospital in Vancouver in 1931, the youngest of the four children of Moses and Sarah Antone. They christened her Velma Doreen, but she was never called anything but Mazie. Moses Antone was a member of the Squamish Nation, which was formed in 1923 when sixteen Coast Salish Aboriginal communities in the Greater Vancouver Area, Gibsons Landing, Howe Sound and the Squamish River watershed amalgamated as a band in order to speak with one voice and improve conditions for the people. Moses was proud to be a full-blooded Indian. "Today," he told his daughter, "not many people can say that they are full-blooded, but I am. Nobody can take that away from me." Sarah Antone's father was Chilean, but he died when she was just ten so she had grown up within her mother's Squamish family.

At the time Mazie was born, the Antones lived on the Capilano Reserve, *Xwemelch'stn*, which lies along the north side of Burrard Inlet from the Capilano River to Ambleside. In those days it was an underpopulated reserve with just seventeen families—most of them directly related to the Antones—living close by the water where the Lions Gate Bridge and Park Royal stand today. The roads were unpaved, and life there was harsh, but this was the worst of the Great Depression years, and things were certainly no better off the reserve. The District and City of North Vancouver had gone into bankruptcy, both employment and money were

Mazie believed that the amalgamation of the sixteen Coast Salish Aboriginal communities signalled the beginning of the demise of the "old ways" and its hereditary chiefs and the move towards the "white" style of government with its elected council. This photograph shows some of the Squamish Chiefs who signed the amalgamation document. Photo: North Vancouver Museum & Archives (#4835).

scarce in the big city across the inlet. The government was sending jobless men to relief camps around the province to build roads and paying them about ten cents a day, and by April 1935 the unemployed rebelled, congregating in Vancouver to demand fair wages and jobs.

Mazie recalled that:

> I guess they were really hard times when I was growing up, but when you are young, you don't notice these things. I know my mom always told me, "We had really hard times when you were a baby, and we lived on fish-head soup for months." Maybe that's why I don't like fish today. Mom and two of her friends had this little skiff, and they would row over to the Vancouver docks where they had a lot of fruit stands. And the owners would throw out the rotten apples and oranges and bananas they couldn't sell, and everyone would go there — not only Natives but whites as well — and some of the stores would throw in a couple of good oranges and apples, too. Mom and her friends would collect boxes of this thrown-out fruit and vegetables and row all the way back to Capilano to share with the other families. I really admired my mom for that. Everyone was so happy to have the fruit, and it didn't matter that it was bruised. They would go home and cut off the rotten parts and eat the good parts. I was telling this to one of my granddaughters, and she said, "Nan, stop it or you're going to make me cry. It's so sad." I told her that we were happy because we didn't know we were poor. We were happy to have the good part of that rotten apple or orange.
>
> We thought we had the whole world when Christmas time came around. Mom told me she had a dollar and she spent twenty-five cents on each one of us. We got a toy, a Jap [mandarin] orange and a few candies. Dad told me that one Christmas when we were older — I think it was 1936 and I would have been five — and he

Mazie spent her childhood on this small reserve under the watchful eyes of her parents, Moses and Sarah. Despite this she still managed to get away and pull her siblings into her battles before being caught. Photo: North Vancouver Museum & Archives (#1452).

was working by then, he arrived home with our presents stuffed in a pillowcase and tried to sneak into the house while we were sleeping. Just as he was coming in, my brother Jimmy was going to the outhouse, so dad dropped the pillowcase on the front porch and walked in without it. Jimmy spotted it on his way back in and hollered at the top of his voice, "You girls, get up! Santa's here! Santa came and left our stuff out on the porch!" We jumped out of bed, ran downstairs and started digging for our presents. Dad just sat there and laughed. He knew he was never going to get the stuff in that pillowcase under the tree now. These are the things that bring back good memories of my brother and sisters. We were really close to one another — especially after we beat Jimmy up!

Big smiles from a young Mazie and her crew of friends and brothers. Mischief seems to be on the agenda. Back row from L-R: Bob Campo, Mazie Baker, Jimmy Antone. Middle Row L-R: Allan Cordocedo, girl unknown, Jack Campo. Front: Roger Antone. Photo: Jack Campo.

Jimmy was kind-hearted, but he used to bully my sisters and me quite a bit when we were young. He would strap us and punch us all the time. So one day Mom and Dad went out to visit her sister, and my grandmother was minding us, and we were so tired of him beating us, so I said to my sisters, Mildred and Vi, "You hold him down while I punch him." My sister Mildred is really quiet — she won't hurt a fly. Vi is between me and Milly and sometimes she gets hot-headed but mostly she is gentle. But not me! I'm what you'd call an orangutan! So they grabbed him and held him down, and I was punching him, but when we let him go, he was so mad he came after us with whatever he found, and we had to climb up a cherry tree just to get away from him. We stayed up in that cherry tree for a couple of hours because we were too scared to come down. Then Mom and Dad finally came home and we got down, and she said, "What's going on?" And we told her what happened.

My grandmother was really mad at us, and she said to my mom and dad, "You should punish those girls because they beat up their brother!"

And my mom said, "He deserves it. He is always after them, and it is about time they did something to him."

My dad just laughed. He was always laughing about things. He had a good sense of humour.

According to family lore, Mazie could be a challenge for her parents as they tried to channel her energy and keep her occupied. Her sister Vi recalled that, although Mazie was the youngest in the family, she was always the ringleader:

She was full of energy, bright and always curious about everything, but a bored Mazie was a force to be reckoned with. Once Dad and Mom were heading off in the truck to visit Dad's aunt in Musqueam. We were told in no uncertain terms we had to stay home. Mazie, of course, decided this wasn't fair. She was going, even if the rest of us kids weren't. Mom said, "No, you have to stay home like the other kids." The truck started up Capilano Road followed by a very determined Mazie, running as fast as she could, shouting, "I *am* going! Wait for me!" Dad slowed the truck and Mom called back to her, "You are *not* going. Go back to the house!" Mazie just kept on chasing that truck. Dad started to leave again, only to see his youngest daughter still tearing after them, face scrunched up with sheer determination. She was not going to quit. She was going to run until they stopped and put her in the truck.

They finally gave up and stopped for her. Dad just laughed and said, "If she isn't going, we aren't going." Mom was mad and she got out of the truck and got a switch off the cherry tree and whacked her on the back of the legs before she got back in the truck. Mazie didn't care, though, 'cause she got to go with them. She was so stubborn. She gets her teeth into something she thinks is unfair and never lets go until it's changed.

Mazie's comment on her sister's story?

Well, I guess I haven't changed much. I bow to nobody. You have to stand up for what you believe in. This is the kind of person I am. I was always stubborn, always determined that things, whatever they were, had to be fair.

Dad always managed to put food on the table and clothes on our backs. He was a proud man and a hard worker, a real handyman. He built all our homes and he could fix anything. He fixed his own cars, never put his cars in a garage or anything. Somehow he always managed to find some kind of work, sometimes logging up in Squamish. When there was no work around here, he'd go up the mountains and look for trees he could carve boat knees out of. That's wood that's shaped like an L, then it's fitted in the bow of a boat. He would lug them on his back all the way down to the mouth of the Capilano where we were living and put them on a skip, tie the skip to the back of the canoe and paddle over to Vancouver. Then he would carry it up to sell to the guys on the wharves — boat builders. He was a hard-working man.

He believed everything he did had to be done right. When he was ten years old, his mom died and he built her coffin; that was when he learned to work with wood. Years after that — in 1968 — our first longhouse burned down, and he designed a new longhouse. He would make a blueprint of what he was going to build. He only had a grade three education, like my mom, but he was the smartest man I know. He wanted a grant from the government to build the longhouse, so he went to Victoria with his blueprint to show them where all the money was going to go. There was no money to be paid out to laborers. Everyone came and donated their time,

Mazie (R) and her sister Vi reminiscing about the scrapes Mazie got them into. Photo: Kay Johnston.

Moses and Sarah Antone. Mazie's parents were both strong people, proud of their heritage. Sarah especially fought for fairness in all things.
Photo: Family collection Keith Nahanee Jr.

and me, Mildred, Vi and my mom cooked for everybody that came to help. My dad said there were people who came from Lummi, Nooksack, Chilliwack, the Island, Musqueam and Capilano. Everybody donated their time. All the money from the government went into the building material. It was finally finished and opened in 1971 when I was forty. Sadly it burned down on April 19, 1980.

When we were little, Dad built each of us our own little bench, and when we went to visit somebody or go to a funeral or an important meeting where you were not allowed to make any noise, we had to take our benches. We were not allowed to get up and run around like other kids. We knew those benches were the only place we could sit. We had to sit there until we were ready to come home. Sometimes it was a long time and we would get numb bums and start wiggling, then Dad would tell us we could go outside to play for a little while, but when we came back in, we had to sit on those benches again.

He was always very strict with us. We were not allowed to go off the reserve by ourselves. We didn't know what Lonsdale [North Vancouver's main street] or Vancouver looked like. It was only when we were in our teens that we were allowed to walk across Lions Gate Bridge to Stanley Park, and then only if there was a bunch of us. We were allowed to go to movies sometimes, but there still had to be a bunch of us. We couldn't go by ourselves, and we had to be back right after the movie was finished. My dad was stubborn, and when he said we had to do something, that was what we had to do. There was no negotiating. We tried, though.

2

The construction of St. Paul's Indian Residential School — sometimes known as St. Francis Indian Residential School — at the end of the nineteenth century was organized by the Roman Catholic bishop of New Westminster, Paul Durieu of the Order of the Oblates of Mary Immaculate. He began the project by inviting the Sisters of the Child Jesus, founded in 1667 in Le Puy-en-Velay, France, to send four of their members to North Vancouver to assist with the development of a school. They were then to stay on to teach the children, incorporating the tenets of the Catholic faith into their lessons. In 1897 the federal government sold the Sisters a piece of land on the Mission Reserve, *Eslha7án*, and they opened a school there just a year later; St. Thomas Aquinas High School now stands on that site in the 500 block of West Keith Road. Initially St. Paul's was supported by donations of food and supplies from the Squamish Nation, but this ended in 1900 when the Department of Indian Affairs took over its administration. The government's goal was assimilation of the Native people into the white colonial culture, and there was, of course, no better place to start than with the young children. No respect was to be paid to the children's language or culture; if they did not speak English or if they practised any of their traditional rites, they were to be severely punished.

In 1920 the *Indian Act* was amended to make attendance in residential schools mandatory for all Native children aged seven to sixteen years of age, although some children entered St. Paul's as early as four. The majority of the students in the school came from the villages of the Squamish Nation or *Sḵwx̱wú7mesh Úxwumixw* along Howe Sound, the Squamish

River and the north side of Burrard Inlet, but some students came from the Burrard Band, *Tsleil-Waututh;* the Musqueam Band of South Vancouver; the Mount Currie Band, *Lil'wat;* the Sechelt Band, *Shishalh;* and the *Stó:lō* Band in the Fraser Valley. Based on existing photographs, it would appear that approximately seventy-five students were in attendance at St. Paul's at any one time, and between 1889 and 1958 when the school was finally closed down over two thousand First Nations children had been forced to attend. The building was torn down in 1959.

Mazie knew that sooner or later she would be taken from her home on the Capilano reserve to St. Paul's, just as her brother and sisters had been before her. When the police finally arrived to take her in 1937, she was almost seven years old and had never been separated from her parents. In old age she still recalled how devastating this event had been:

> I was scared and angry. I just knew this was wrong and unfair, and I made this very clear to the Sisters by just refusing to cooperate.
>
> I remember being in school there for less than a year — maybe just three or four months — I'm not sure how long it was. I remember sitting at a desk but I don't remember writing or doing anything with books. I didn't learn how to read or write. My sisters and brother hated school, too, but they did their time and learned to read and write.
>
> I don't know if I was just plain stubborn or that I just didn't like school, but I tried my best to be difficult. Stubbornness was my way of fighting things I didn't want to do or if I was scared. I just wanted to go home. My sisters tried to protect me from beatings, but I challenged the Sisters dozens of times a day. Like my mum said, "Once Mazie gets her mind set to something, there's no way anybody's gonna change it!"
>
> I remember we sat at this big long table — must have held about thirty kids — and they'd bring the food and say, "Here's your supper. You eat it." And I'd say, "I don't want it." And they'd push it back at me and it would go

on and on. And then the nuns would say, "If you don't eat it, you're gonna get the strap." To me, if I didn't want it, I didn't want it. I didn't like boiled sausages and cabbage. They would shove that plate at me and I would shove it right back. My sister Mildred would give me her empty dish and take my full dish and eat what I didn't want to eat because she knew I wouldn't eat it and I'd get a good lickin'. She'd be throwing up trying to eat all that food.

At lunchtime we got a thick slice of bread we could put jam and peanut butter on, and that was okay. We never got any fruit even though there was a big apple tree on the walk from St. Paul's to the chapel … it was like a five-minute walk … and there would be apples lying on the ground, and if anybody picked up one of those apples and ate it, they would get the strap from the nuns. They just didn't want you to have them and they would rot on the ground …

We slept in a room on the second floor, like a ward, where there were maybe six or eight beds. The little kids, like the seven- and eight-year-olds, were in one room, and the older girls had a bigger dorm. They had to look after the younger girls. Sometimes at night I would get scared and want to go home and I would wet the bed. You got the strap if you wet the bed. At the end of the hall there was one small room and that's where one nun would sleep to keep an eye on the kids so they don't get out at night … or run away. She would check on us … I remember the flashlights coming in the night … so Mildred would try to hide the wet sheets before the Sister came through and saw what I had done. I was so miserable and scared being away from my mom and dad.

We started the day with a dose of cod-liver oil. It was really thick … like syrupy … and all day long I could taste it. I remember eating porridge in the morning, and then there was making your bed and putting your clothes in the closet — we had to wear a uniform during school hours. And then we'd go down and either do dishes or mop the floors or something. They had a yard full of swings and merry-go-rounds and teeter-totters and that was what we did at lunchtime … They didn't have any games for the kids except gymnastics, but I wouldn't do it. After school we had to do our chores. The older girls had to look after the younger kids, but they had to do the laundry, too. We all had a number that we had to have on our clothes so they would know which matches to who so that our stuff didn't get mixed up. We had long black socks we had to wear — I hated those things! — with our number on them. The younger ones, like me, mopped floors or did dishes; the boys did all the cutting of wood and splitting it.

The children were required to speak English at all times, but this was no problem for Mazie as she knew no other language:

My dad never let us learn the [Squamish] language because of what he went through — he was punished so much. He didn't know any English when he started at the school, and they would slap him, rap him on the knuckles with a ruler, hit him on the back of the head with a book. They would put him in a corner … kneel him in the corner and he had to have his nose against the wall, and if he moved his nose from that wall, he would have to kneel again for another four hours. He said that the nuns didn't understand that the kids didn't know how to speak English. He told us about all the little kids from all the different reserves who didn't know any English but were punished if the nuns heard them talking to each other in their own language. Some of the kids had never even heard English before coming to school, but they still got strapped if they spoke their own language. That was just not fair.

My dad said he would never let us go through that. So when we were growing up, he never spoke the [Squamish] language, not in the house. Not ever. And my grandmother would speak to him in the Squamish language, but he would speak to her in English because he didn't want us to learn it. He could speak it but he wouldn't … and his job on the docks called for English so he gave up his language. My mum understood it but she didn't know how to speak it.

So that's one thing I never got in trouble over at school because I always spoke English. I was fluent like my brother and sisters. To this day I can't speak or understand my own native language.

Parents could come and visit their kids but they couldn't take them home. Mom would take us out for fifteen or twenty minutes for a drive up Lonsdale or a walk. My brother would put up a fit when he had to go back. He'd hang onto the telephone pole or whatever he could grab onto. I think that is what really killed my dad … just having to leave him there.

Sarah Antone, however, was not in the least intimidated by the school or the Sisters.

So she came to the school, brought us bread, peanut butter and jam and fruit — bananas, apples, oranges — which the other kids didn't have. And we had to sit in a classroom to eat what we got from our parents 'cause the other kids didn't have any. My mom brought our own clothes up 'cause after school classes you could get into your own clothes. But Mom come to visit us one night and we had on these raggy old clothes, and she was so upset. She said, "My kids never ever had clothes like that!" And you know, each time she came, she found something wrong. Maybe a week or two went by, and my mom came back and she said, "I would like to see my children."

And the nun said, "No, you're not allowed to see them."

Mom said, "Well, I'm not leaving. I want to see my children."

I guess the nun got tired of her waiting there 'cause she went and got us. Me, Jimmy and Mildred come to the door, and we sat and talked to our mom, and when we kept scratching our heads, Mom said, "What's the matter with you girls — always scratching your heads?"

"It's itchy," we said.

Then she looked in our hair and we were just full of bugs. "Next time," Mom told the Sister, "I better see my kids in their own clean clothes with clean heads. My kids have never *ever* had head lice!"

The Sister told her, "Your kids are well looked after here. We cut their hair to prevent lice." Mom was not impressed with that answer — after all, her kids *did have* head lice. Then the Sister snapped, "It is no wonder your youngest daughter is such a problem — she's just like her mother!"

So the nun told us to go to our rooms, and my mom left and she came back the next week, and we were still scratching our heads. And Mom told us all to go upstairs and get our own clothes, but when we came down, the Sister is standing halfway down the stairs with her arms spread out and she said, "You're not going anywhere!"

Mom said, "Look, if you don't want to be laying in a ball at the bottom of the stairs, you'd better get out of my way 'cause I'm taking my kids home, and there's no way you're going to stop me."

The Sister moved out of the way 'cause she knew my mom was a fighter. So my brother Jim got his clothes and met us out by the gate, and we walked out that gate and we never came back.

Mom told me later that she would go to see the Indian Agent and he'd say, "Here comes Sarah — we're in trouble now! What did we do today, Sarah?" She'd say, "When I get there, you'll find out." She had the Department of Indian Affairs on their toes every time she went over there. I guess it was easier than having a fight with her. That agent knew he would lose anyway. But everyone respected her—they called her Ma—everyone on the reserve, you know. And those Sisters found out pretty soon that she wasn't gonna let them tell her what to do or stop her from seeing her kids.

3

Within days after Sarah Antone's confrontation with the Sisters at St. Paul's Indian Residential School, the police turned up at their door. They gave Moses so many days to return his children to the school or he would be sent to jail. Mazie recalled:

> My dad said, "I'm not letting my children go through what I went through. I don't want them going through all that prejudice." That was my dad.

So Moses and Sarah packed the family's belongings onto the roof of their old car and headed south across the border into Washington State. It was 1938, and Mazie was seven years old.

> My dad had a car — I don't remember what make it was … maybe a Model-T. And you know how you see in the old movies how they tied everything on the fenders and the back of their cars with ropes? Well, Mom would fill up boxes with our clothes, bedding and stuff, then she would put all our dishes and pots inside the zinc bath tub and it all went on top of the car. And when we got all settled in, that would be our bath tub. We looked like the Beverley Hillbillies travelling down the road.
>
> Once we arrived in Washington State, the whole family worked from late May to October picking fruit, vegetables and whatever there was to pick. You name it, we picked it — blackberries, raspberries, strawberries,

After running away from the residential school to Washington State, the family worked in fields like these picking berries. It was back-breaking work. Seattle Post-Intelligence Collection, Museum of History and Industry, Seattle, Washington State, USA.

cherries, apples, plums, currants, beans, corn and hops
— from Bainbridge Island to Vashon Island, to anywhere
there was work. We'd stay away maybe ten to eleven
months out of the year, and then we would come home
for a month, stay in our home and then take off again to
the States. Did that for years.

The farmers provided tents for us, and with all six of
us in our tent, we had to pitch in and keep it clean and
tidy. When we went to the States, I was too young to
work on the grounds with my mom and dad and I had
to stay home and clean the tent and cook. Later the only
one thing I never picked was strawberries 'cause there
was snakes in those patches and I am deadly afraid of
snakes — and mice too — so I had do most of the chores
during strawberry season. My dad said if you can't get
out and work in the fields, you have to do the work at
home. So strawberry season was not my favourite 'cause
I didn't like doing all those chores. We took turns washing dishes, doing laundry and cooking ... well, Jimmy
didn't cook, thank goodness ... but even in a tent Mom
and Dad still had their strict rules for us. We were not
allowed to run around and spend our wages on treats.
Dad told us we had to save our money so that we could
buy clothes for the winter in Seattle. We were expected
to pay for most of our own clothes because we had made
money all summer.

Moses planned the family's picking season, setting out when the new
crops were in bloom to make sure the family would be hired at the farms
with the best berries. The farmers were always pleased to have the Antones back each year because they were all good workers and they were
reliable.

We knew everybody because we saw the same people
every year. It was like family. Other people would have
to work until five to pick what we made by noon. The
carriers had little baskets — six in each one — and when

that carrier was filled, you put it at the end of your row, and my brother had to carry them to the shed where they punched our cards.

We made good money and life was good and we had fun after work. It was way better than school.

My dad was a very strict person. Us kids, we had rules to go by and we never disobeyed his orders. I don't ever remember getting into trouble — maybe I did — I don't know, but as far as I remember I always did what my parents told us to do. He trusted us and through that trust we could do what — well, almost anything. Like we'd go to movies after picking berries all day, and in the evenings we'd walk about a mile to the coolers to get a Popsicle. Or Dad would say, "We made our money for the day. We'll go swimming." A whole bunch of us would pile into our car, and we'd head for the closest swimming hole. It was a great way to cool down after all that dust and picking. We would go dancing sometimes. I loved to dance — I still do!   and pickers would often get together and have a dance somewhere in a barn or an empty field if it was dry weather. We sometimes had to travel six or seven miles on dirt roads to get there. There were times we could only go so far by car and then had to walk the rest of the way. By the time we got there our shoes and clothes were full of dust. I didn't care. I danced until all the dust fell off.

Hop picking, which ended in October, was the Antones' last picking job of the season. Mazie's sister Vi remembered Mazie playing tricks on the other workers:

> To make money we had to fill I don't know how many sacks — lots and lots of them — because the hops were like feathers, they were so light. We'd cut the tops off, strip the vines, take all the leaves off, pick the hops and put them all in a big sack that was weighed so our ticket could be punched. The plants were really tall, higher

than this ceiling—maybe ten feet. The hops were at the top and the only way we could reach them was to wait for the boys who came along with long poles with hooks on the end. They would hook the wires off the posts so the hops would fall to our height, and when we finished picking, one of them would follow behind and hook them up again. While we waited for the boy to come and put the wire up again, Mazie would hide in the vines, then sneak out and hang onto the wire. The poor boy wasn't able to get the wires back up on their posts. The other boys came back to see what was happening. "What the heck is going on? Why can't we get this wire back up? It should be lighter than this." They were so puzzled.

Mazie finished the story:

I was there hiding, waiting for them to try again, then I'd let go and they'd go flying. Boy, were they mad! I could run faster than they could, though, and I would dash back to our tent. By the time they got there, we were all laughing. I tell you, we had fun.

By the late 1930s most of the farming operations in Washington State were gradually becoming mechanized, and when the farmers brought in machines that shook the plants to make the berries fall off into containers, they needed fewer hand pickers. However, some of the pickers were trained for new jobs, such as working on the machines and in related jobs in the machine shop and in the new packing sheds. Moses, Sarah, Jimmy, Mildred and Vi got jobs working on the new machinery or in the packing houses, but Mazie was too young to be allowed near the machinery—much to her annoyance. "I had to stay home and cook and do the shopping *and* keep the tent clean," she recalled.

When the picking season ended, the family packed up the old Model T again, loaded the bath tub onto the roof and headed for Seattle, where they lived in an apartment on Jackson Street for the winter. Mazie, still too young to get a "real" job, worked part-time in a corner grocery store that belonged to Filipino friends and did a lot of babysitting to make money.

Moses got a job in the shipyards each winter, and he came home one day in January 1940 with the news that the first Canadian armed forces had left Vancouver for Europe and that the shipyards in Vancouver were building corvettes and mine sweepers for the Navy. Mazie's older sisters and brother were more aware of the war effort than she was because in the winter they all worked in factories or on the docks, listened to the news on the radio and read the newspapers. For Mazie, however, the war seemed far away:

> I knew there was a war going on. I listened to my mom and dad and their friends as they talked about the warships being built and soldiers fighting and being killed in Europe. Everyone was on edge.

Despite this and their gypsy-like existence, the family had stability in their lives. They made good money, always working at the same picking camps with the same families in summer and moving back to the city to the same apartment and the same jobs in the fall. They continued to do this until 1945, seven years after their cross-border escape, when Moses felt it was finally safe for them to return to their home on the reserve. He figured that the police would no longer be interested in harassing the Antones about their kids not being in school and little danger of Moses and Sarah being put in prison for non-compliance.

Mazie recalled her dad telling her that the world was safer too because World War II in Europe was over, and atom bombs had been dropped on Hiroshima and Nagasaki, causing Japan to surrender and removing the fear of invasion along the West Coast. He said they would be going home and that there were even a few supervised local dances she would be allowed to go to with approved friends and her older sisters — as long as they were back by a set time. To Mazie, being allowed to go to a real dance hall, not a barn in a dusty field, was the most exciting part of all this news.

It would be good to be home again. Their home on the Capilano Reserve had stood empty but watched over by friends all the time they were in Washington State.

4

The Antone family began looking for work on the Vancouver waterfront as soon as they were resettled in their home on the Capilano reserve. Moses was quickly hired as a longshoreman, while Sarah, Jimmy, Mildred and Vi found jobs at the home plant of the Canadian Fishing Company (Canfisco) at the foot of Gore Street in Vancouver.

These were busy years for British Columbia's fish canning and processing industry. Salmon canning and herring reduction were the primary activities, and while some of the processing was now carried out by fully automated machines, workers were still needed to cut and prepare the fish for the cans, jobs that required manual dexterity, speed and accuracy because very sharp knives were used, and one slip of the knife and a finger was gone. The work was both difficult and repetitious, it was carried out in a noisy, fast-paced environment, and the plant was cold and wet for much of the year. However, the jobs were secure and they paid well.

Mazie was still underage when her mother and older siblings started at Canadian Fishing, so once again she found work babysitting, but as she was considered very reliable and responsible, she was never without work, sitting for her aunts and anybody else who needed her. However, as soon as she turned sixteen in 1947, she was hired at the cannery.

> My mom, Mildred and Vi were already working there so I went to work with them. We used to catch the ferry at the foot of Lonsdale and it landed at the foot of Columbia Street on the other side — two blocks from the cannery. It was five cents to go over and five cents to come

back. That first year was a blur. It was really hard 'cause I had to learn so many new things. And the first thing I noticed was that this working for a living really cut into my social life. By the time I arrived back home, had supper and did my chores, there was no time left until the weekend finally arrived, for meeting my friends, playing basketball, riding my bike and dancing. One thing I do remember that year is the wedding of the Queen — she was still Princess Elizabeth then — and Prince Philip. I think it was sometime in November.

The salmon fishing season lasted three to four months, and during this time the fresh fish had to be processed as soon as the fish packers arrived with their catch, so the cannery workers' day was even longer. Sometimes, Mazie recalled, they had to work Saturdays and even Sundays:

> It was all work, work, work, but I made a lot of money to spend later. I went through every job there was in the cannery. I worked in the warehouse, I washed fish — they cut the heads off and let them run up on the belt, and the women that weren't tall enough to reach the belt had to stand on these little stools. The water would be running and you'd be cleaning and you had to throw the fish onto the belt. I worked up in the can loft, too ... in that can loft, boy, if you didn't have enough sleep, you'd fall asleep on the job 'cause the cans came out so quiet you could just doze off. Finally I moved to filling cans, and I realized I could pack cans *really* fast. I was good at it. From then on I did piecework like my mom and Mildred. Pieceworkers did an 8 to 5 shift and I would get home way sooner than Vi 'cause she didn't like piecework. It was way too fast for her. She said it was scary with all those fast-moving knives chopping up the fish.
>
> The line we worked on we were standing so close to each other, and everyone had to stay within their boundaries, but nobody ever wanted to work beside us Antones because we were the top fillers in the cannery — my

mom, Mildred and myself. We were moving too fast. My cousin tried to do it, but she was grabbing empty tins and throwing them on the trays, and she said, "You just make me too nervous. I can't do it."

We filled the tins by hand so we wore gloves, and they wouldn't issue you new gloves unless they were completely worn right out. And sometimes we'd go through four pairs in a day — me and my mum and sister — because we were so fast. Our heads were covered with white kerchiefs to keep our hair away from the machines, but — it drove you crazy — so I wore white flannel diapers. They never slipped off your head. Some of those ladies would get done work and their kerchiefs would be all lopsided. And we wore aprons, and ours were so long we had to fold them and then tie them.

The fish were cut into steaks and sent down to us in boxes. We took the steaks from the boxes and put them on

Mazie hated the head coverings at the cannery because they kept slipping off; instead she wore a diaper that stayed in place. Her kids had fun giving her a hard time about her diaper head. Photo: Mazie Baker family collection.

our table, slit the tails and cut off the fins. Those knives were really sharp, and you had to watch you didn't cut your fingers. We had our own knives, and I made sure mine was real sharp, otherwise it would chew up the fish and it would be wasted. We fitted the steaks in the cans by wrapping them around. If it was too much for the tin, we would have to cut off all the extra bits but you couldn't waste anything. So the machine would throw off any can that was too light, and we had to fill it up with smaller pieces so that it was tight and the right weight.

We would have to fill forty-five cans—I think they were quarter-pounders—to make eleven cents. For every forty-five tins we got one punch [on our cards]. We used to make $33 a day so you can imagine how many tins we did a day to make that much. That was big money in them days, and the longshoremen used to say to my dad, "An- tone, how come you're working? Your daughters and wife

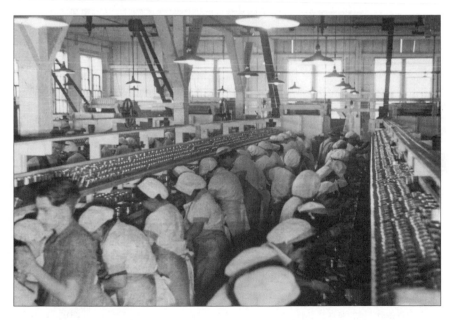

Women with their flying knives on the high-speed production line at Canfisco. Mazie kept her knife sharp to prevent it from tearing the fish.
Photo from the collection of the Canadian Fishing Company.

make more than you do—you don't even have to work!"
'Cause together me, Mildred and my mom made $99 a
day. He just laughed and kept on working.

Some of the other workers were mad because we
were the top fillers, and they said, "They are not doing it
properly. Their tins are too heavy … too light …" Even
when they knew the weighing machines would kick off
the cans that were too light or too heavy. So what the
boss did was he came and brought us a scale and he said,
"You have to weigh every tin you fill." And my mom said,
"We don't have time because we are using our time to
make money." And she said, "You come stand here and
you weigh every tin you need to weigh." And every tin
that we threw to him was right on. And he said, "Ah,
to heck with it." Some of those women were jealous. It
wasn't our problem now, was it? We just knew when a tin
was too heavy or too light, we were so used to doing it.
The other women just grunted, but they never said anything about our work again.

We used to get our pay in little brown envelopes because we never had time to go to the bank when it was
open. But then the women started complaining because
instead of giving us the cents they would keep them, and
that's a lot of pennies over the years. The women said,
"So where do all those pennies go?" So they had to give
us the pennies. And then they started giving us cheques,
and I had cheques in my wallet for months before I could
get to the bank.

One of Mazie's cannery stories is a reminder that the stubborn little
kid who had refused to be left behind by her parents was alive and well and
working in the cannery! Apparently the foreman's girlfriend worked on the
same hand-filling line, and he always treated her with what looked to Mazie
like favouritism. One day this woman spilled fish on the floor and walked
away without picking it up. The foreman came along, saw the fish lying on
the floor and told Mazie to pick it up. She told him in no uncertain terms

that she had not dropped it and she was *not* going to pick it up. He persisted … foolish man! He was not going to win this because there was no way Mazie was going to pick up that fish. Finally he left with the fish still on the floor, and shortly afterwards his girlfriend returned, angrily picked up the fish and stomped off. Mazie smiled and just kept on filling her cans.

After the salmon fishing season closed and all the fresh fish had been canned and shipped out, the workers moved over to the cold storage area to work on frozen fish such as sole and tuna, which was stored there in huge stacks. They had to cut up the fish and pack them head to tail in long boxes; once the boxes were full and at the right weight, they were put on a conveyer belt and sent down to be sealed. The Antone women couldn't make as much money doing this as the workers were only paid a flat rate of eighty cents an hour, but it was still good money for those days.

Canfisco had made history back in October 1909 by being the first to ship frozen fresh halibut by train from Vancouver to the New England Fish Company in Boston. To keep the fish cold, they had installed a second set of walls inside the railway cars, and inserted huge slabs of ice into the space between the walls. At sidings along the way the train would stop long enough for the ice to be replaced, but the fish arrived safely in Boston and declared as fresh as the day they were caught. The success of that first trip opened up a whole new market for BC fish on the other side of the continent. In 1936–37 the company brought in equipment that would freeze the fish even faster, improved the insulation in their plants in Vancouver and Butedale, and increased production of ice and ice storage. By the time the Antone family came to work there, it was a source of great pride for the workers to know they were working for a company that was recognized as the most modern in the world — after all, even the Queen knew about their salmon. Mazie recalled:

> I worked on hand-filling smoked salmon for the Queen
> when she came to visit. That was a real exciting time. We
> even had special labels made for her.

However, eventually the cannery became so mechanized that there was no longer a need for pieceworkers, and Mazie moved on to the Queen Charlotte Cannery, which stood where the Bayshore Hotel stands today, next to the entrance to Stanley Park. She quit her job there in 1958, after

Many years after working on the canning line for Canfisco, Mazie visited the home plant to search the archives for photos for her biography. Photo credit: Tony Van, corporate photographer, Canfisco.

working in the canning industry for eleven years. By then she was married and had two children and wanted to be home with her family.

In October 2009 Mazie, who was now in her seventies, returned as a guest to Canfisco's home plant to go through the archives and select photos for this biography. She was met by Jocelyn Smith, who had arranged for Mazie to meet with Don McLeod, vice-president of Canfisco, in his executive office. Mazie regaled him with stories of her years at the plant and told him how her mom's career there had been written up in the *Fisherman* magazine when she retired in 1975. He asked if she would provide him with a copy for the company archives and then if she would agree to having her photo taken by the company's photographer, Tony Van, for the company news-letter. She beamed as she followed Tony down to his studio for the photo shoot; later one of those photos took pride of place in her living room.

Going through the company's extensive photo files took several hours, but fortunately Jocelyn Smith had previously located possible selections from the company's archival photo collection. Mazie, commenting as she looked through them, spoke as if she could see the machines, feel the knives, hear the people again; she described hand-filling the cans at high speed, what she wore on her head, which knives she used. She had gone back in time, reliving it all.

Afterwards, Jocelyn took her on a tour of the plant. Although it stood empty, Mazie was able to point out where she had been stationed and which machines she had worked on, talked about getting up early to catch the ferry across the harbour and walking to the plant. At the end of the visit as Jocelyn accompanied Mazie out to the car park, she told her she had learned an amazing amount listening to her, too. Mazie left the plant flying high, and driving home across the Second Narrows Bridge, she announced:

> I still can't believe a vice-president took time out of his day for me! My mom would never have dreamed that her daughter would be talking to a vice-president in his own office and having her photo taken in that special room. And how about that Jocelyn — imagine all the time she spent before I even got there and then she even showed me round the plant!

5

After the commercial salmon fishing season was over each year, Mazie had her weekends free to be a teenager.

> There was a whole bunch of kids all the same age on the Cap reserve. We would walk over to Stanley Park once in a while. We always walked over and walked back because we never had the money to catch the bus. There was six or eight of us.

However, their favourite destination was the hall on Third Street on the Mission Reserve — the Old Hall as it was generally called — where she and her best friends, Betty and Harriet Nahanee, went for basketball and dancing.

> I guess today we would say we were "hanging out." One night we would all go to "Indian dancing" and on another night to "serious dancing." Serious dancing to me was jiving. Oh, I loved dancing! I could go to a party and dance all night. A lot of them had to be drinking to go to a party and dance. Not me! I don't like booze — I just wanted to dance. I still like to dance, though my jiving isn't what it used to be. My knees just won't bend the same!

In those days there were no shopping malls on the North Shore where young people could "hang out" — the first stage of Park Royal was not built until 1950 and the Capilano Mall opened in 1967 — but there were

Mazie (R) and Mildred in their teens dressed up to go to the movies. Photo: Mazie Baker family collection.

two movie theatres on Lonsdale — the Lonsdale and the Odeon — and admission was just five cents. All of the girls loved the movies, though the film was not as important as being out with a bunch of friends. And things improved after Harriet Nahanee got her driver's licence and the use of a car. At last they could head off into unsupervised territory, and it was exhilarating.

The three of them often went to bingo where Mazie won the jackpot so often that people at the bingo hall would joke: "We may as well all go home now — Mazie's here!" This did not deter her in the least. "Hey, ya don't think that was gonna make me lose on purpose, do ya?" Laughing she recounted one of their bingo escapades.

> The three of us were running late for bingo one rainy night and we ran to get into the hall before we got too wet and missed any games, and well, wouldn't you know? Harriet dropped her car keys in a muddy puddle. We were there digging around for the keys and couldn't find them. Harriet says, "Oh, let's leave them — we're gonna be really late for bingo. We'll get them when we come out." We left them somewhere in that puddle and went in and played bingo — I can't remember if we won anything. Probably did. When we came out, we searched for those keys and finally found 'em, got in the car, started the car and what had happened? We had a flat tire! So the three of us took the wheel off, and Harriet said, "You girls wait here while I roll it down to the gas station. It's not far." So we waited and waited; she was gone about forty minutes. She finally comes back and says, "Sorry it took so long but the guy was busy." We put it back on and got in the car ready to go, but something was still wrong: the back tire was flat! We're standing there in the rain just killing ourselves laughing. We had to go through it all again. I said, "We'd better check the other two tires before you go back or we're gonna be here till tomorrow." We just couldn't stop laughing and we were soaking wet. That is how we were — me, Harriet and Betty.

Like Mazie, Harriet grew up to be a fighter for their people and the land, though when they were in their teens, it would never have entered their minds.

> It just sort of happened as we got older and began to understand what was happening to our land and our people. Harriet was arrested in May 2006 for blockading the construction of the Sea to Sky Highway at Eagleridge Bluffs. They said it would improve travel to Whistler for the 2010 Olympics. They didn't care that it was our land. She was 71 and they put her in prison for fourteen days in January 2007. We could not believe it. Putting an old lady, a respected elder, in prison. Disgusting! The Nation was in an uproar over the disrespect shown to our elder. Harriet filed an appeal, but she died not long after she was released from that Surrey Pretrial Service Centre. It was all so sad. She was my friend almost all my life. We had such good times together when we were younger. No, we would never have even guessed that we would become so political. We didn't even know what political meant then.

Although Mazie and her sisters all enjoyed socializing with their friends in those days, Mazie was the member of the family who was into sports, especially basketball; she was fast on her feet and, although she was small, she could sink baskets from a fair distance. They played in the Old Hall on Third Street, which was used for all kinds of events including birthday parties, but most importantly it had a basketball court painted on the floor. It was while playing there that Mazie began to notice Alvie Baker. She had known him by sight since the day about five years earlier when she and her sisters had gone to the Mission reserve to rescue their brother, Jimmy.

> About four of them jumped my brother, and they were going to beat him up. I was maybe twelve at the time. Anyway, they grabbed him and threw him to the ground, and when we went to pull them off him, they yelled at us,

"You Capilanos, get outta here!" One of them grabbed
my sister Mildred's shoulder from behind to pull her
away. She had long nails, and she just went down on that
guy's hand and just ripped the skin all along the top. But
they never picked on Jimmy again. I guess from then on
they knew that we were fighters and we wouldn't let anybody push us around. Like my dad always said—you
have to speak up for yourselves … even us girls.

Alvie Baker, needless to say, had not really caught her eye favourably
that day. But one evening in 1948 when all the teenagers were at the
Old Hall, he noticed Mazie and caught her watching him. She laughs,
remembering:

Well, I was hard to miss—I was kinda rowdy. Alvie was
a quiet, kind and gentle man. I guess I wanted a quiet
husband 'cause I was rowdy enough all by myself.

Mildred, meanwhile, had caught the eye of another young man
from the Mission reserve, Norman Natrall, and the sisters started dating
at the same time. As they did everything together, their parents decided
they were now "grown-up" enough to be allowed to cross the Lions Gate
Bridge and go into Vancouver with their dates. They began teaming up
with other young couples as well, and sometimes a group of them would
walk over the bridge to go "uptown" to the theatre—the Strand, Odeon,
Vogue or Capital.

Although 1948 was a big year on the West Coast—this was the year
of the big Fraser Valley flood, Vancouver switched from street cars to
trolley buses, North Vancouver city came out of receivership—Mazie
was more interested in the newest music and dancing. Crooners were
not her favourites as their songs were not really good for jiving, but she
did recall Bing Crosby bringing his Philco Radio show to town that year.
His song "Hair of Gold and Eyes of Blue" was a big hit, but not great to
dance to, and she was stunned when the Squamish Nation made him an
Indian chief.

Why on earth would they do that? Even I knew he wasn't
gonna do anything for us. He hadn't done anything to

deserve such a huge honour. I guess someone on council was star struck.

Early in 1951, almost three years after Alvie and Mazie, Norman and Mildred had started dating, Alvie and Norman proposed to the sisters. Mazie was now twenty and Mildred twenty-four. Before proposing the two young men had come up with the idea that they should get married on the same day and have one big wedding. The problem was that they were scared of the girls' father, Moses, and they told their prospective brides: "You need to go tell your dad that we want to get married."

So me and Mildred went upstairs — my dad and mom's room was upstairs in the house — and knocked on their door. I said, "Can we talk to you?"

Dad said, "Yeah, come in."

We sat on the bed and told him and mom, "We need to ask you something. Alvie and Norman would like to marry us, but they are too scared to ask you, so they sent us to break the news."

"Nope, they will have to come and ask themselves. I will not let you ask for them," was Dad's answer.

I asked if they could come by the next night and sit in the parlour with them and ask.

My dad acted tough and told me they could come and try.

Oh, they came, and they were so nervous. Alvie's hands were sweating. My dad didn't make it easy for them; he told them to wait downstairs while he and my mom talked it over. Finally dad said I could marry Alvie because he was a hard worker and had worked since he was young, but he didn't know about Mildred marrying that Natrall boy. My mom jumped in and told him if he was going to let his youngest daughter get married, it wasn't right to stop Mildred getting married. He should let us both get married at the same time. I think dad gave in after we went downstairs because, when they came down, they said we could both get married.

That wasn't the end of it, though. Alvie had to go and ask his parents if he could marry me because he wasn't twenty-one yet. His mother said, "No." She told him I was too spoilt, and we were so rich I would want expensive clothes and everything nice, and he wouldn't be able to give it to me. His dad stepped in and told her, yes, he could marry me because I was a good worker and I would be really good for him. Poor Alvie, he was so nervous listening to them both, but he told his mother he would be twenty-one in six months and she would not be able to stop him and he was going to marry me anyway. His dad and mom must have done the same as mine and talked it over, but it was his mom who changed her mind, not his dad. We did get married and, yup, we got married in a double ceremony. We were married on December 1, 1951, and Alvie and me were together forty-two years until he died in 1993; we had nine kids, so I guess we worked out okay. I don't have any photos though. They were all lost when our house burnt down.

After we had been married for a while, Alvie's dad told his wife that he had been right: I was a good worker. I always had laundry on the line, my house was clean, I split wood when we got a big truckload and stacked it so the wind could blow through and it would dry faster. I worked steadily at the cannery, and I didn't drink.

Mazie Antone was now Mazie Baker; she soon had a home on the Mission Reserve and a family of her own. This new focus and its responsibilities proved to be the catalyst that gradually channelled her big heart, her sense of fairness and no-holds-barred outspoken manner into a force to be reckoned with as a mother, wife, and later as an advocate for her family and the Squamish people.

6

In August 1958 the ferry that had carried the Antone family to work at Canfisco each day ceased operating; it would be another nineteen years before it was replaced with the Seabus. But Mazie's reasons for quitting work at the Queen Charlotte Cannery that summer were far more personal: although her daughters, Gloria and Brenda, were now in school, she also had a new baby, Tammie.

> I worked for a while, but finally I quit working 'cause there's no way I could work and not be wondering if my family were being taken care of. Who was looking after them, who was feeding them — if they were getting fed. I told my husband that I can't work and worry about my kids at the same time. He said, "Then quit your job, May. We don't need your payday. We can manage on mine." So I quit. I had eleven years seniority in the cannery.

It was true that at that time Alvie and Mazie were in reasonably good shape financially as Alvie was working full-time at the M.B. King Mill. Mazie recalled:

> After I quit, we didn't have the best of everything. My kids didn't have the best clothes — I got a lot of them from the Salvation Army and I bought clothes for them on sale, but they weren't in rags. They were always clean and fed. Today I see mothers struggling to bring up just one kid, and they call it hard work; they have

wipes, disposable diapers, food in jars, formulas already made — it's a breeze. When I had to wash clothes by washboard, my hands were half-raw wringing them out by hand and hanging them on the line. I had five clothes lines and they were always filled. I'd be washing pooey diapers out and hanging them out on the line in the wintertime and bringing them in so stiff I'd have to hang them inside to get the frost out of them. There was only coal oil lamps, no electricity and no running water on the reserve. But that was our life. We did what we had to do to survive.

In the mid-1960s the Baker family's house burned down. Mazie's eldest daughter, Gloria, recalled:

Mom and Dad had just come back — I think they had been paddling with the War Canoe Club — when someone spotted smoke coming from our house. Fortunately no one was hurt but we lost everything. Mom was upset about losing all her photo albums, all the photos of us when we were little, the ones of her when she was little and her wedding photos. We had to live next door at my dad's mom's house until Dad built us another house. We had no clothes so Mom, Aunty Mildred and Auntie June Baker would go to the Salvation Army thrift store every Tuesday and get us new clothes. They would come home with all these paper bags and we would all dive in, digging around, pulling out all the new stuff and choosing what we wanted.

By this time the Baker family had grown in numbers. After the births of Gloria (Honey) and Brenda (named after singer Brenda Lee) at the beginning of the 1950s, there had been a large gap before the family expanded again. Tammie, named after singer Tammy Wynette, had arrived in 1958, eight years after Gloria; Alroy (Roy or Bucky), named after the football star Elroy "Crazy Legs" Hirsch, was born in 1960; Alvie Junior arrived in 1961, Shawn in 1962, and Karl (Beck) in 1964; Leah (Tia) was born in 1965; and finally Bert arrived in 1969.

Mazie raised her family in exactly the same way her parents had raised her. She was strict, she had rules, and they were obeyed. She said:

> Bringing up nine kids wasn't easy, but it's not hard once you teach them "no." Once they're six months old, they learn it right away. Most people say, "Don't say no to your children," but that's what's lacking today. The kids don't know that word "no." I don't think it hurts them. I always said no to my children, and they grew up fine. And I didn't have to tell them NO, NO, NO all the time. I said no once and that was it. They understood no means no. I'd tell them there are two words that are easy to say — yes is the easiest word and the other is no, and that is the hardest one. When you grow up and somebody says, "Do you want a cigarette?" you have the option of saying yes, and it's going to be hard to say no. Same if you go drinking. Nobody will be twisting your arm.

Gloria has vivid memories of her parents' rules, though it was her mom who ensured they were followed:

> We didn't have any money to go anywhere when Brendy and me were little. We'd walk around the rez on the beach where the marina is now and watch the men take out the canoes and practise for the races. I would push Tammie in her stroller and run as fast as I could on the gravel road so the stroller was kicking up stones. There was no way we were allowed to leave the rez by ourselves or even with friends. One time Teresa Baker, Brendy and me sneaked off and went down between Chesterfield and Lonsdale where there were big chestnut trees; we climbed into the trees and had fun shaking the branches so the chestnuts fell down. We lost track of time, so it must have been getting after supper, I guess, when Mom came down to get us. "Get down here!" she shouted, and then she gave all three of us a whack. "Get home now!" We moved pretty fast. Teresa never forgot that day.

✦

The first of the children to leave the family home was Gloria, who was injured in a car crash just before her sixteenth birthday and placed in a cast from her waist down. When she was released from hospital, it was decided that it would be better for her to stay with her grandmother, Sarah Antone, as all the other kids were still at home. She was happy to go there as it meant having space for herself as well as more independence. But best of all was getting away from helping with the family laundry.

Then on January 31, 1972, the M.B. King Mill declared bankruptcy and closed. Suddenly there was no money coming in, and Mazie and Alvie, with nine children to feed and clothe, had to make major changes in their lifestyle.

> We got piled in bills because they didn't honour the cheques coming from the mill. So Alvie went logging, did whatever he had to do to find work. And the kids and me stayed on the reserve while he was out in the logging camps. And I just couldn't handle it. So when he phoned home, I said, "I can't stand it, being at home by myself with the kids. I don't feel safe. I need you to come home." So he came home.

Mazie's dad, Moses, had been a longshoreman for many years, and Alvie decided this was a job worth having, even though he knew it would be hard to get full-time work on the docks. But he was patient and determined; he would arrive at the hiring hall at 5:30 every morning and stand in line until 6:00 at night to be available whenever extra men were needed. Work came sporadically at first, but after eleven years he was finally working full-time and eligible to join the union. The money was good and things became easier for the Bakers:

> As my kids grew up and my husband got more work, we would take the kids out for burgers and fries … there were only seven of them at home now because Honey and Brendy were already out on their own. And they learned how to share everything. They would have half a fries each and half a hamburger and half a pop. They

never complained. And to this day they still share with each other. If one is not working and the others are working, they will say, "Here, bro or sis, here's fifty bucks. Don't worry about paying me back." That's what sharing has taught them. And I look at them today and think, I must have did something right when I brought up those kids. I'm a real proud mother. I think I have the best kids going. I *know* I have the best kids going.

All of the children remembered the family picnics, even if it was just down the road to the water's edge. Sometimes the picnics were on their own lawn with a sprinkler going so they could run under it to stay cool, making a hot summer day bearable. But the best picnics were to places like Alice Lake. The car would be packed in the morning with kids, food,

Mazie's nine children. Back row L-R: Alvie Jr, Karl (Beck), Alroy (Bucky), Shawn and Bert. Front row L-R: Leah (Tia), Gloria (Honeygirl), Tammie and Brenda (Brendy). Photo: Family collection, Keith Nahanee Jr.

and lots of towels, and they would be gone for the whole day, coming home exhausted, ready to fall into bed. All of them remember the family trip to Disneyland, their first major trip away from home as a family. Tammie, who was by then the oldest child living at home, hadn't wanted to go because her younger brothers were going and she was "too old" for this kind of thing. But she did go and was surprised when she really enjoyed herself. Mazie had the brilliant idea of putting a small wading pool in the back of the family station wagon and filling it with cold water so the kids could take turns cooling off in the heat while they were on the road. They stopped at gas stations to buy ice to throw in the pool, and they camped on windy beaches with Tammie holding the tent down while Mazie hammered in the tent pegs. When they finally arrived, it took them a while to find a motel that could take all nine of their family and the carload of friends travelling with them. Everyone, even the adults, went on the rides, screaming and giggling. All of them still talk about this trip.

Mazie's lack of schooling had made her determined her family would be educated. Gloria and Brenda had begun first grade at St. Paul's, which by this time was run as a day school by the Sisters of the Child Jesus. Gloria, who found the school "dark and stinky," completed grades one to three there, and part of her education included European folk dancing classes; she became a member of the St. Paul's Dance Troupe, which travelled to competitions as far away as Disneyland. Mazie made all of her costumes. After St. Paul's Day School closed its doors in 1959, the two girls transferred to Queen Mary Elementary in North Vancouver School District. The seven younger Baker children began their schooling there, though later overcrowding at Queen Mary resulted in them moving to Westview Elementary.

It was her children's schooling that involved Mazie in one of her earliest forays in activism; she demanded that the band council provide a bus to take all the reserve children safely to school:

> I had to fight for a school bus for my kids because after school people would rush around [in their cars] and not watch for the kids on the road. So I felt so much safer when I got the school bus, and every kid went to school when

they had that bus. But after my kids grew up, the council dropped the school bus, and I had my granddaughter Sarah starting school, so I went back and fought for that bus again. One of the councillors said, "It's going to cost us a lot of money to get that bus going." And I said to him, "Are you saying to me that my granddaughter is not worth the money you pay for that bus to pick them up?" He shut his mouth and he wouldn't say another word. So we got that school bus going again, and all the kids were on that bus going to school. But today there's no bus running and half of the kids don't go to school. And our band doesn't realize that this is what they need because a lot of them have to walk a long way to school.

But the school bus was only a start. When Mazie and her sister Mildred got tired of the cabs and milkmen and anybody else who delivered on the reserve "just ripping through there" and endangering their children, they went back to the band council and asked for speed bumps and signs telling drivers to slow down. This time council didn't need too much convincing as many of them had experienced near misses as they walked along the roads.

Mazie was thoroughly involved with her children's education, going to their schools to introduce herself to school principals and classroom teachers and to give them very clear instructions regarding the treatment of her sons and daughters. If any of them were in trouble of any kind, she told them, she was to be contacted immediately.

I told them, "Just call me and I will be there as fast as I can. You are not to do anything until I get there. I don't want my son or daughter being interviewed without me being there. If they have done something wrong and we all decide something needs to be done about it, I will make sure that it is. I just want my kids to be treated fairly."

One day Shawn's teacher sent him home to bring his mother to school. When Mazie arrived, she was told Shawn would be suspended for two weeks because he had been fighting and that the fight was his fault.

Immediately Mazie asked, "Why are the other boy and his mother not at this meeting?" The teacher replied, "It was not the other boy's fault." Mazie asked, "Have you listened to both sides of the story?" The teacher's response was "No, but the other boy would never start a fight." Wrong answer. Mazie was *not* pleased. "I will come back when this other boy and his mother are here so we can all hear both sides. That will be fair. Until then my boy stays in school." There was no follow-up meeting with the other boy and his mother, and Shawn stayed in school.

When one of her kids skipped school, the school would phone Mazie and she would track the culprit down. Then she would lay down the law. Alvie recalled his mom telling him that, if necessary, she would take him to school, holding his hand, and stay there with him all day, every day, to make sure he stayed — even tying him to his desk if necessary. Alvie said:

> I knew she would do what she said, and all my friends would make fun of me for having my mom come to class with me. Without hesitation I told her, "Mom, I swear I'll go to school every day." Mom and the teacher teamed up to keep a check on my attendance, and it miraculously improved.

Mazie and Alvie were so proud that all of their children continued on to high school. Tammie and Roy (who became known as Bucky) attended St. Thomas Aquinas Catholic High School, which was established on the site of the old St Paul's Residential School, while Alvie, Shawn, Bert and Tia went to Hamilton High School. Karl started high school at Hamilton but later switched to Carson Graham. Mazie recalled:

> When my son Roy graduated from St. Thomas Aquinas, I went up there with my dad. My husband wasn't much for going to things like that — he would rather stay home and watch the kids. So my dad would come with me to see my kids graduate, take pictures of them and tell them how proud we were of them.
>
> Karl was always in special grades, and he graduated from Carson Graham. Then he went to Capilano College and he graduated from there. When I went up

to see him graduate, he said, "Mum, you know I'm the only son that graduated twice." And he laughed. "That's right, Mum?" he'd say. And I'd say, "Yeah, Karl, that's right. You're the smartest one." And he'd laugh. "Yeah, Mum, I know."

His name was Karl but everybody called him Beck. He was loved by everyone on the reserve. He would go collecting bottles to go to bingo. He'd start early in the morning — even though he got his money from welfare, he would still go out collecting. "No, I'm going out to get bottles today, Mum." I'd say, "It's raining out!" and he'd say, "I'm all right, Mum!" People would have their bottles waiting for him ... have them in bags waiting for him. They said, "Nobody else gets these bottles but Karl." And that's how he made his money to go to bingo. He enjoyed his bingo.

Karl never ever left home. He was always here with me. He would poke his head in the door and say, "Hi Mum, you need anything from the Mohawk's today? You want me to get you some nuts?" And I'd say, "No, Karl." "Are ya sure, Mum?" "Yeah, I'm fine, son, thank you." And off to bingo he would go ...

Karl died in a street accident in 2006. He was 42. Mazie recalled:

He went to bingo one night and he got hit at Second and Lonsdale. He died ... I don't know exactly what happened, but he was standing in the middle of the traffic lanes, I guess. I don't know if he backed up and slipped off the sidewalk. That car just happened to come up and hit him.

He passed away before I could get up to the hospital — they came for me and I went up there and he was already gone. And the doctor said, "Would you like to donate his organs to a bank?" We gave them everything but his eyes. My daughters said no, we won't give up his eyes. So we got a letter from the family of the guy that received one of his lungs, and it was such a beautiful letter saying how thankful they were that he got his lung. And we got a letter from a mother that had two young girls, and she said if it wasn't for your son's lung, I would not be living today, and now I'm going to see my children grow up. And it was such beautiful letters that came to us from her husband, her mother, her father and herself. That's the way my son was — always giving somebody something.

He was a wonderful son. All my kids are wonderful.

Mazie passed her enthusiasm for sports on to her children.

I like all kinds of sports, and I always try to get my kids and grandkids into sports. I think they are the best gift anyone can ever give a kid. Keeps them out of mischief and well behaved.

All of her boys played football, baseball and hockey. The girls played softball and soccer, and Tia was into jogging and would spend time at the track. As well as basketball, Tammie loved to roller skate with friends on Fridays at the Stardust Roller Rink on Marine Drive in North Vancouver, which operated from the mid-1960s to the early '80s.

Alvie and Mazie were always at the boys' football games. Logistically this was a challenge as they were all on different teams, and all of them played at the same time on Sundays. They would drop one off, drive to the next game and drop off the next one and the next one; then they would drive back to the first one and catch some of the game, then on to the next one until they had managed to see something of each boy's game. Tammie recalled:

We had one TV in the house and my dad, mom and brothers all watched sports. I learned all the rules for football and hockey. People would ask me if I played, and I would say, like no, but I have five brothers.

However, baseball was probably the major sport within the family. Alvie and Mazie made up a team of their own kids and others from the neighbourhood and drove them to the games in their van. They were gone all day Saturday and sometimes, when they were in a tournament, most of Sunday as well. Mazie took along Kool-Aid and jugs of water, plus all the makings for sandwiches — ham, mayonnaise and mustard — so the kids could make their own when they had a break. But the best thing for all the kids was that they had uniforms. Mazie had gone to Value Village when she heard they had baseball jerseys on sale for 99¢. She bought a selection of different sizes and gave them out at the next game. The kids looked great and felt like a real team, and they were absolutely convinced they played better because of their uniforms.

As always, Mazie had rules for the team members. They had to be prepared to show up for practices because, she told them, to play well as a team you had to practise as a team. Alvie, who was their coach, would take them down to the field and put them through batting and running practices and teach them fielding strategies. They all knew they had to be at the van at 9:00 a.m. sharp to be ready to leave for their game; if they were not there, too bad — they were left behind. They were not allowed to play if they had been drinking the night before, and they had to have respect for each other. "They all learned about respect," Mazie recalled, "respect for their team members. They had to learn to work together." And it all paid off. They became such a good team that one year they won the championship of their league and brought home the cup.

Tammie recalls her mom always being there for her baseball games and encouraging her and the rest of her team to practise, practise and practise.

> I knew that it really showed when we were out there playing. When we lost, there was no "dressing down" or blaming. Instead we were told to focus on the next game and to play the best game we could.

However, one of Tammie's favourite mom stories concerns a mothers' and daughters' basketball game she helped to organize as a fundraiser while she was in high school.

> I think it was in 1974 or '75. I had recruited my mom, and the other girls got their moms to come out to help

us raise money to travel. The gym was packed. It was great seeing all our moms out there having so much fun, and we all kept breaking up with laughter. My mom was the smallest on the team, but boy, was she fast! She ran circles around everybody. She could dribble the ball, go down there and do a layup like you would not believe. I really enjoyed being on the same court with her. I'd watch her and say, "That's my mom!" And guess what ... the mothers won and Mom was declared the all-star high scorer!

As well as her love of basketball, Mazie had been an avid paddler in her younger years, travelling with her teammates, Ruth Seward, Hazel Baker, June Baker and Corny Brown to competitions with their canoe, *St. Teresa 1.* But after she married Alvie, they became members of the War Canoe Club.

Me and Alvie were very involved in paddling for years, which meant we were often away travelling to canoe races in Duncan, Lummi, Chehalis and Cultus Lake. We loved it but eventually gave up competition paddling, but Tammie and the boys were involved by then, and we were right there cheering them on.

I remember when Bert wanted to join the canoe racing teams when he was 13 or 14. He tried his best for two years to persuade me to let him join. I always said no because the canoes used to go out under Lions Gate Bridge, and I was scared he would drown. But when he was 16 he just went ahead and joined anyway. And to top it off, he was the bowman, and there was one race where he jumped out of the canoe ...

Bert continued the story:

Our canoe got stuck 'cause it was a new canoe that was square on the front instead of round like usually. And the bow got stuck on the starting line. The rope coming back dug into the wood, so I was trying to hit it with my paddle to get it loose and it wouldn't come loose. So I had to jump out and pull the rope off the canoe, and the crew pulled away without me.

And Mazie finished the story:

And the canoe started coming back, and his father said, "Where's Bert?" He's not in the canoe!" And my heart was just exploding. But he was in the water, and it's lucky the crew coming behind didn't hit him in the head 'cause those canoes come full force.

Roy Baker took up ocean-journey canoeing, which had been the Squamish people's method of travel from village to village in the old days. In time many of these trips became ceremonial or commemorative and lasted several days so Mazie and Alvie would follow the boats by car down the coast. Roy recalled:

She would show up where we pulled in for a rest or to stay overnight and bring clean socks, underwear and clean t-shirts; she knew we wouldn't be able to do laundry because we were in the canoe all the time. She made up packs of clothes, clothespins, Band-Aids, Tylenol, and lard to suck on if we got a sore throat. It always felt good to look at the shore as we were coming in and see Mom and Dad waiting and encouraging me when I was so tired from pulling paddles for hours in heavy ocean water. But that's how they were with all of us. Always there for us, encouraging us to be the best we could be.

7

Mazie had experienced little contact with Squamish culture in her youth, but she had been drawn directly into it in her thirties when her dad, Moses, decided to give her an ancestral name. In the *Sḵwx̱wú7mesh* culture names are very important and are handed down through many generations. They can only be passed down through a blood link so are usually taken from an ancestor of the same family and are given during a traditional naming ceremony. These ceremonies are usually a big event and a source of pride, but this was not the case for Mazie.

> I felt so out of place because, when they spoke the language, I didn't know what they were saying. Then they did a lot of the culture, which I didn't know either. It was, like, embarrassing for me in front of my own people. It all felt so strange. I had to learn how to say my name; it was hard for me to do 'cause I had never heard it before. But once I got my name, I was so glad because it was my dad's mom's name: *Yenyansemaat-t*. It had come back to be given to me, so I was still attached to her through her name. My dad said it was not really done in the old way because in the old way you had to go out yourself and invite people to come to the ceremony; you don't phone them and ask them.

Ceremonies in the longhouse created problems for Mazie, too.

> I can't go to longhouse for the ceremonies or anything. The floor is bumpy and my knees don't like that; then

there is the smoke and the dust, and sometimes the feathers are still there. I'm allergic to all of them. I'm allergic to everything in the longhouse. How embarrassing is that! And on top of it all, I don't like salmon!

Gloria, Mazie's eldest daughter, was the first of the family to move back into the Squamish culture, inevitably drawing Mazie into it, too. At eighteen, Gloria attended a gathering in the Capilano longhouse, and one of the elders, Ed Brown, a medicine man, saw how affected she was by the drumming and singing and told her that she had to "go into the longhouse, *milha7a'wtxw*, (the dancers' house)." A family meeting was called at the home of Sarah and Moses Antone with Gloria's parents and paternal grandparents in attendance, and Brown told the family that, if Gloria didn't go into the longhouse, she could die. Although Alvie, Mazie, and their children had not been involved in any of the old spiritual customs pertaining to the *Skwxwú7mesh* culture, they were aware that going into the longhouse was a lifetime commitment. It would also be costly for the family as they would have to buy blankets and prepare food and pay others to teach her, and Gloria would have to stay in the longhouse for something like two and a half months while undergoing the intensive spiritual experiences and learning the ancestral ceremonies before she could be made a member of the Longhouse Society. She would then spend her winters travelling to ceremonies throughout the Northwest, teaching others who had lost the knowledge of how to speak the language, follow the protocols and perform ancient ceremonies such as memorials. Mazie recalled the tense family discussions at that time:

> Alvie and my dad told Gloria, "It is too hard. It is a hard life. The old-timers used to save all their money in the summer to go and do their winter singing. You will have to pay someone to come and stand beside you, to sit you down and drum and sing for you. You will miss your family in the wintertime because you'll be so busy travelling." Alvie did not want her to go. There was no way he wanted Gloria to be in longhouse. We didn't know anything about what it took to be a dancer. We didn't know the training they had to go through because, like I said, our

dad would never let us learn our culture and our language because he went through so much by knowing all that. I told her I don't have the money so I can't say yes or no to you. Sarah and Margaret, her grandmothers, were in favour, though, and finally all the family agreed that Gloria should be allowed to go into longhouse and become a spirit dancer. Alvie, Moses and Margaret came up with the money to support her throughout her initial hard training.

When her training was done and she was ready to come home from her stay in longhouse, we brought all of her brothers and sisters down there. And she was sitting around the fire with her guardian sitter, and when my kids seen her and the way she was dressed … the paint and the hat … they up and screamed and ran out the door. It had been a long and hard spiritual journey. She had to dance every morning, learn how to get strong, not be afraid or holler at the sounds. She had to find her own song and know how to drum before she could leave. I don't know her song. It is hers and nobody else can sing it. We were just so proud of her. I can't sing or drum. I didn't know anything much about longhouse. I still don't. But I know now that her training didn't finish when she came out. She will go on learning all her life.

Gloria was still quite young when she came out of longhouse, so Mazie would accompany her on her travels because the ceremonies often lasted until the early hours of the next day. There was no way she was going to have her daughter travelling alone so late and so exhausted. Mazie recalled:

One day Gloria came out of the house, ready to go to longhouse — there was a long staircase coming down from the sundeck — and the mailman just happened to be coming up the steps. Of course, [spirit dancers] go out backwards, right? … I think it's because some spirit could be coming in and it could hit you if you're facing it. And then they turn around at the door, and when she turned around and he seen her in her paint and her hat, he just threw the mail at the door and he went down those steps like you wouldn't believe! And he was saying, "Don't hurt me, please!" But if you've never seen a dancer, it would scare the heck out of you. Another time we were coming back from Musqueam at about four o'clock in the morning and we had Gloria in the back seat in her *temlh* (longhouse paint), and we stopped at the stoplight, and there was a milk truck beside us, and he just happened to glance over and he froze. He seen Gloria in her longhouse stuff, and that light went green and he was still sitting there. I bet he was wondering what the heck is that?

She is called in so often to teach the ceremonies and help families carry out memorials, but it is a hard path teaching the old ways, and I was nervous about this part of the longhouse. You gotta watch when you are putting on a memorial because there is a lot of crankiness going on — people are fighting each other about whether they should do it this way or that way. I didn't want her getting into the middle of that kind of stuff. You never know what could happen. I made sure that I travelled with her until, of course, Keith became a member of longhouse.

Keith Nahanee, who became Gloria's husband, entered the longhouse after she did to become a mask dancer, and together they spent their winters travelling, celebrating in the ancestral ways and teaching the ceremonies to those who had forgotten or never knew them, but also to work with alcoholics and addicts. However, after they had children, Mazie became concerned about the amount of time they were away from them, and she talked to Gloria about finding a better balance between longhouse and family. Recognizing the impact of their absences, Gloria cut back on travelling until her family was older, and at that time she and Keith returned to their longhouse commitments, Keith as a mask dancer, and Gloria as a *stelmith* or spirit singer for the mask dancers.

Gloria also expanded her cultural involvement into a new beginning for an abandoned tradition — the powwow. There had been powwows on the Capilano reserve in the 1940s and '50s, and Mazie remembered them lasting for as much as ten days:

> Sy Baker was the one that held those powwows at Humalchsun Park, down at Capilano. People came from Saskatchewan, Alberta and Montana, and the park was full of teepees. The longhouse was full of arts and crafts and we could watch people making baskets, carvings or beading.

But gradually the elders who knew the traditions of the Squamish powwow retired and died, and the last of these annual events was held in 1958. Exactly thirty years later Gloria attended a community meeting to propose the revival of the powwow. As she sat in the circle waiting for her turn to speak, she was nervous as she was not used to asking for support for a personal dream. It was not an easy sell, but she told the people that she had been told by the "old spirits" that they wanted the powwow revived, and she persuaded the chief and council that it would benefit Squamish youth to be involved in a drug- and alcohol-free activity and introduce them to some aspects of their heritage. A year earlier she had organized the Squamish Nation Dance Group, consisting of fifteen children, including her own daughters, Kanani and Riannon, and taught them the traditional songs and moves that she found recorded on films made in the 1940s and '50s. This group now became the centrepiece of the revived event. Today the Squamish Nation Powwow has grown into one of the largest, most successful annual events on the North American powwow circuit. It is held at Humalchsun Park, the same site as those long ago powwows, during the second weekend of July, and well over two hundred dancers plus drummers and singers from all over Canada and the US participate. More than four thousand visitors attend from Canada, Europe (especially Germany), Australia and the US.

From the start Mazie was involved in the Squamish powwows by providing moral and practical support to her daughter and by applying her sewing skills to make dance regalia for her granddaughters. However, she was also enlisted to make bannock for sale at these events, and Mazie's bannock soon became famous far beyond the realms of her own home and family. Years earlier, when her children were young, she had taught herself to make it by trial and error, although her first attempts had produced something akin to rocks. Undaunted, she had persevered until finally one day she began serving up golden brown, light as a feather bannock.

Then in the mid-1980s when Gloria had staged a mini-powwow to give her own daughters, Tammie's daughter, Sarah, and some other young dancers an opportunity to dance in public for the first time, she had asked her mother if she would make bannock to sell at the event. Since it was to be held in the field beside the longhouse, she could use the longhouse kitchen, but Mazie was hesitant. She had only ever made it for her own family, and she was convinced no one would buy it. But Gloria was very persuasive, and finally Mazie agreed. On the day of the pow-wow Gloria put up a small sign that said: "Bannock: 50¢ @ piece," and Mazie was in business. To her surprise a lineup formed and grew longer and longer. She was making fresh bannock as fast as she could, but as her hands were constantly covered in dough and flour, she couldn't handle the money as well, and she had to ask her customers to produce the correct change. After their first taste, no one complained about the wait or the inconvenience of having the right change, and they happily lined up again for seconds and thirds.

As this first powwow was just a one-day event, she only made about fifty pieces of bannock, but the ensuing powwows were much bigger events, and as they continued to grow, it became impossible for her to make enough by herself. She moved from the longhouse kitchen to her own kitchen and enlisted the help of family and friends.

> I would mix the bannock, Margaret [Canute] worked at the opened-out [dining] table covered in plastic bags to protect it. She'd throw flour all over it, then I would come and flop the new mix down and she'd make the patties. Then she put them into six electric frying pans. Wendy [Lockhart] would do the cooking, turn them, change the oil and lift them out when ready. Together we would make about 150 an hour. We packed 'em in big boxes,

> layered and separated by clean towels, and sent a truck
> down the two miles to the powwow concession. They
> kept running out of bannock down there. I never did get
> all my towels back. I have no idea where they went!

On the powwow grounds word would spread quickly when the truck loomed into view — some people claimed they could smell the fresh bannock as it left Mazie's house. It sold out almost as soon as it arrived, but no one seemed to leave the lineup, preferring to stand chatting while they waited for the next delivery. Some even tried to buy from the delivery man before he reached the concession, a strategy that was not well received by those standing in line.

Then one year the Squamish Band office received a phone call from the Aboriginal Peoples Television Network (APTN) asking if the Nation had a good bannock maker. Mazie was unaware of this phone call until her own phone rang and she was invited to be a guest on the Rick Harper Show to demonstrate how she made her fried bannock. She asked how on earth they had found her and was told that someone in the band office had said she was the very best. Mazie accepted their invitation and, accompanied by her daughter Tia, flew to Winnipeg to tape the show.

> I had to cook at Rick's house because the studio wasn't
> really equipped for a cooking show, and the cameras and
> all the other sound equipment had to be brought over to
> his kitchen. I had decided to make Indian Tacos for the
> show, but they disappeared so quickly — eaten by Rick
> and the crew — I was worried there wouldn't be any left
> for the actual show. Then there was a call-in for view-
> ers as part of the show, and I answered questions from
> all over Canada about bannock problems. That was so
> much fun. It was the best part.

Afterwards friends from both inside and outside the Nation called to let her know how much they enjoyed the show. "I felt like a TV star just because of my bannock!" Mazie is frequently asked for her recipe by people who have tasted her bannock, and she is happy to share it with everyone.

Mazie making thousands of pieces of bannock in her tiny kitchen. The "Best in the West" according to the cooking show she was invited to on APTN. Photo: Kay Johnston.

Mazie's Bannock Recipe for a Powwow Weekend

(exactly as dictated)

20 twenty-pound bags of Five Roses Flour (<u>no other kind</u>)

6–8 giant bottles of cooking oil

4–6 tins (the biggest ones) of Magic Baking Powder

water

Equipment

6 Electric frying pans. (They will only last for one powwow weekend. You will need new ones for the next time!)

Measurements

This is the tough part. It is all done by the "feel" and by the handful. Just keep adding flour, baking powder and water till it feels right. Good luck!

Instructions

Mix the water and flour thoroughly or it won't cook in the middle. Stringy dough means not enough water.

Don't play with the dough too much; the less you touch it the better it comes out.

It's all in the hands. Pay attention to how it feels. Don't punch it down because that makes the bannock heavy.

Once it starts to fluff up, you have to cook it right away. The oil has to be very hot. Turn them over when they are a light golden brown. They should come out nice and light.

Serving suggestions

Spread with butter and jam

Use as a taco base for Indian Tacos

Side serving with chili

Salmon on a bannock

It is best served fresh when it's hot/warm. You want to make fewer than 4,000 bannock? It is a math thing! (You may have to add a calculator to the equipment list to work out what you need for a more regular-sized batch.)

In more recent years Gloria worked at the *Eslha7áń* Learning Centre in North Vancouver, teaching a cultural program called *Chun Es7a7awts* (or Yes, I can do it) for Native children who were most likely to disappear from the school system by Grade 8. She also developed a pilot program called Sea and Sand, which with the help of her brother Roy was translated into *Sk̲w̲xwú7mesh snichim.* The children learned about respect for themselves, their elders and others. Most of these students eventually returned to their schools and stayed to graduate. Unfortunately, after a few years, funding for this program was cut from the Band Council's Education Budget.

Other family members also became involved in the traditional Squamish culture, especially the revival of the language. By the time the St. Paul's Indian School closed in 1959, the Squamish language — or *Sk̲w̲xwú7mesh snichim* — had almost entirely vanished, exactly as the federal government had intended when they passed the *Indian Act.* However, during the 1950s a Dutch linguist named Aert Kuipers, who had been teaching at the University of BC, became interested in it and spent long hours talking with those elders who still spoke it among themselves, and as a result, in 1967 he published a 400-page dictionary and grammar book. It was a first step toward saving the language, and in 1973 when linguist Randy Bouchard and anthropologist Dorothy Kennedy began their BC Indian Languages Project, which was designed to breathe new life into the Native languages of this province, the Squamish elders were among the first to become further involved in order to save their language for future generations. It was Bouchard who devised the writing system presently used for the Squamish language.

Meanwhile, in 1972, two of the Sisters of the Child Jesus approached the band council to ask if someone could come to St. Thomas Aquinas High School to teach the students their people's language. The band council agreed immediately and followed up by asking Mazie's father, Moses Antone, and her uncle, Louis Miranda, and Andy Natrall to donate their time to teach the language at the Grade 8 level. Although Moses had refused to let his children learn the language, he had never forgotten it himself. He had just refused to speak it because it had caused him so much pain. But soon the three men were working with teacher Vanessa Paul at St. Thomas Aquinas — an act that was poetic justice since it was on this site that they had been punished for speaking their language in their youth.

Mazie's eldest son, Roy, and his friend Stewart Gonzales were two of the first students to begin learning the spoken language in Grade 8. Roy remembered it as a difficult process:

> After we got to know a little bit of the language, one of them would ask us what sentence we wanted to make up. We would think of one in English and go up to the blackboard and wait while Uncle Louis thought about it. Then he would tell us word for word what to write down in _Sk̲wx̲wú7mesh_ ... that's how we learned. I wanted my rugby team to learn the language because it would be a real advantage on the field [because] the other teams wouldn't know what we were planning to do.

Roy was surprised when he discovered his own father, Alvie, could speak the language, too:

> I knew he would go over to his mom's after work, and sometimes I'd be sitting on the front porch smelling the yeast bread in the oven as he sat talking with her, but I couldn't understand what they were saying. I found out later they were speaking _Sk̲wx̲wú7mesh_.

Having a father who could speak the language meant Roy could ask him for help with his language homework. He would bring home lists of words and sit down with his dad to go over the pronunciation.

> Dad would look through the list, reading the English and _Sk̲wx̲wú7mesh,_ and come across words he didn't remember having in the language. Once he asked me, "How do you say black?"
>
> I said, '_k̲'exk̲'íx̲_'.
>
> Dad said, "You know, that isn't right. We say _k̲'íx̲_ '"
>
> What I was really saying was black black!

Mazie remembered these homework sessions very clearly:

> Roy would come home and say, "Dad, I want to know if
> I'm saying this right?" Alvie would get really upset. He
> would say, "*NO!* It's not even the same language!" You
> see, it had a different "slur" to it. Randy [Bouchard] was
> the one who put all the 7s [representing glottal stops] and
> Ys in it, and Alvie said they should have spelled it the
> way it sounded. Lots of the elders said the same thing. It
> changed all the sounds. Most of the language came from
> the throat. My dad and Alvie were both brought up to
> speak the language in the old way.

Roy is aware of the controversy and says:

> There is still resistance to the written or new language
> today by some of the very old elders. I remember taking
> part in a ceremony when an elder jumped up and shout-
> ed, "This is not my language. I can't understand a word
> you are saying!" And she stormed out.

Mazie continued:

> Alvie never spoke the language in the house to me or to
> our kids, but he and his mom would talk *Skwxwú7mesh
> snichim* every day. The rest of us who were born in the
> '30s missed learning the language. Me and most of my
> friends, we've lost it. We never *had* it. It's Roy's generation
> that is bringing it back. It's different though, big time. I
> really admire those kids for trying to learn it in school
> now, but it needs to be spoken in the home every day.
> That's not going to happen because the parents don't
> speak or understand the language. Maybe these kids will
> remember and teach their kids so that future generations
> will learn and speak it every day in their homes.

Not everyone in the Squamish band felt the children needed to learn
their Native language, and when a request was made to the band council
for funding to expand the language program, the council turned it down.

This response was not well received by Mazie or her friend Jackie (Nahanee) Gonzales who had backed it. Jackie worked for the band's education department, and her job included overseeing the Parents Advisory Committee, which held community luncheons to let parents know what was going on in the schools. She and Mazie had met when Alvie was skipping classes, and as they began working together on school problems, Jackie had helped Mazie to expand her political understanding and involvement at her local level. So when the band council turned down the request for funding for the language program, the two women reacted strategically. Jackie recalled:

> We decided to try and inform the elders publicly by calling a general meeting to tell them that the council considered the language program a waste of dollars and it was scheduled to be cancelled. The result was that at the meeting a motion was put forward and passed to retain and fund the language program in perpetuity.

General meetings gave the community a perfectly legal strategy for dealing with conflicts between the people and the band council, and Mazie and Jackie had just discovered how effective they could be: the resolution that was passed on that occasion proved to be a long-term benefit to the community and instrumental in preserving the language. Today the band has a vibrant language program in the schools and a Squamish–English Dictionary (‘*Sḵwx̱wú7mesh Sníchim–Xwelíten Sníchim Sḵexwts*’). The Squamish Nation Education Department also offers a web-based word-a-day program of *Sḵwx̱wú7mesh* as well as online classes for at-home learners. Meanwhile, Roy Baker, *K'etximtn*, never gave up on his language; he continued studying the written version in school and eventually became a teacher, teaching the *Sḵwx̱wú7mesh snichim* in Grades K–12. He also takes part in ceremonies where the traditional language has to be used.

Brenda, Tammie and Tia Baker also became involved in their culture by working with youth and families in traditional ways, such as teaching the medicine wheel, storytelling, dancing and performing some of the old ceremonies. Brenda, Mazie's second daughter, became involved with her culture by becoming a winter dancer. Tammie arrived at her chosen cultural involvement after struggling with alcohol addiction for several years and now works with *Soh-sah-latch* in a program called Home Instructional Parenting Program for Youngsters (HIPPY). Tia, the youngest daughter, became a nanny but remained at home.

8

The Antones remained a very close-knit family, even after the children grew up and married. They lived in homes almost next door to each other, moving freely between each other's houses, and kept their doors and arms always open to each other's children. In her later years, Mazie became sad when she spoke of those days:

> It's not the same today with families. They all go their own way and are too busy. Kids don't know who their cousins are anymore, and they don't visit back and forth like we all did. I think they lose a lot of who they are, you know. They aren't helped the same way we were just by being around each other.
>
> My mom was my anchor. I always knew I could count on her. And my dad too. They were there for me and my sisters and brother, and for my kids … big time.

Mazie was devastated when her mom, Sarah Antone, died in 1975. The guiding light in her life had been extinguished.

> When my mom got sick and passed away, that was something I could not handle. It took me years to get over losing her. I was so upset I couldn't look after my kids, I couldn't sleep, I couldn't eat. She was the first one that passed away, the first death I had really close to me. My husband would come home from work and say, "May, ya gotta get up and look after your kids." I'd try, but thank

God, I had him looking after them 'cause I just couldn't. Then one day he said, "May, you *hafta* get up to look after these kids and straighten up." I wasn't drinking or anything like that — I just kept thinking of my mom.

Moses Antone was bereft too; he and Sarah had been married for forty-nine years and they had never been apart. It seemed as though nothing the family could do was enough for him; nothing made him feel any better. He died two years after Sarah. In some ways it was a relief for his family as there was no joy in his life anymore; he pined for Sarah and tended to live within his memories of her and their life together. In some ways Mazie found it easier to let her father go. "I thought, 'Well, this is what you want, Dad. Now you're happy — you're going to be with Mom.'" But she never forgot how much they had taught her.

It is significant that the first major battle outside the reserve that Mazie Baker became involved in occurred in the fall of 1975, as she slowly recovered from the death of her strong-willed mother. The battleground was the section of Third Street in North Vancouver that cuts through the Mission Reserve on a strip of land the band had deeded to the City of North Vancouver for a road back in 1910. As the years passed, this stretch of roadway had become a major connector between the Lonsdale area, the Lions Gate Bridge to the west and the Second Narrows (now the Ironworkers Memorial) Bridge to the east, and because it was the most southerly route on the North Shore, it also had heavy truck traffic going to and from the BC Rail yards on the waterfront. However, on the section of Third lying between Bewicke and Forbes streets, the pavement narrowed from four to two lanes with wide gravel shoulders and ditches but no curbs or sidewalks and no traffic lights. In spite of the congestion here, drivers still treated it as a freeway, speeding through, ignoring pedestrians and throwing bottles, cans and other garbage out of their car and truck windows.

Unfortunately, most of the reserve children had to cross this dangerous two-lane section of Third Street each day to attend school. Finally, a group of Squamish band members that included Mazie, her good friend Jackie Gonzales, Percy Paull and elder Earl Newman went together to ask the band council to make a request to North Vancouver City Council for the installation of a traffic light at Third Street and Forbes. Mazie had not hesitated to join this group:

> I had nine children going to school, and every time we heard a car screech on Third all the mothers would be out on their porches, wondering whose kid had been hit. My heart was up in my throat every time. *Every time*. We would run up the road, all the mothers. I just couldn't handle it. I had to do something, so when Jackie told me what they were going to do, I was in.
>
> This was after our good councillors and chief had passed on, and now there was this new chief and council for our band, and when we went and asked for a [street] light there, they said, "No, we're not going to get into that because it's the white people using that road through our reserve."

This was not well received by the group, and they decided to take more direct action. In preparation, Jackie researched the injuries and fatalities on this stretch of road in the twenty years between the mid-1950s and 1975 and discovered that seven pedestrians had died and another thirty people had been injured there. The issue gained momentum a few days later when a band member, Missie Jones, who was in the ninth month of pregnancy, was hit at Mahon and Third streets by a car speeding through the reserve. Her baby died and Missie's injuries kept her in hospital for a long time. Fatalities now numbered eight and the total injured had risen to thirty-one.

With all this information in hand, Jackie sent a letter to the City of North Vancouver's council requesting a traffic light and outlining the reasons for the request. Meanwhile, the group busied themselves printing pamphlets and making placards in preparation for taking the battle to the streets. With a support group of about thirty people they showed up at the intersection of Third and Forbes at 7:30 a.m. on Tuesday, October 14, armed with their handouts and placards. Mazie recalled:

> I said, "I'm not taking this anymore. I'm taking my kids out of school until they get a light there." So what we

did was ask our kids if they would come out of school
and line up on Third Street and hand out papers to
the drivers that slowed down and tell them why we are
doing this road block. And all the kids from St. Thomas
Aquinas came too and lined up with our kids along the
roadside.

Some of the people were so nice and said, "We understand what you are doing." Others would be swearing
at us, trying to run us down. One young guy came up in
his truck, and he said, "I'm just going to open my hood
and make believe something is wrong with the engine,
just to back up your traffic for you." And we thanked
him and he would stay there about a half-hour fiddling
around with his truck engine, but there was nothing
wrong with it. Then he'd say, "See you tomorrow!" and
away he would go.

The protesters were careful not to block the street but stood on the
crosswalk and along the roadside, handing out pamphlets to those drivers
who slowed down to ask what was going on. But as motorists slowed to
see what it was all about and the picketers answered their questions and
explained why they were picketing, they caused a tie-up that extended all
the way to Lonsdale.

Meanwhile, Jackie had arranged for the group to meet that same
morning with the city's mayor, Thomas H. Reid, to personally present
their requests for safety initiatives on Third Street. It was not a positive experience; Reid treated them aggressively and left them feeling angry and
disrespected. (The archived council minutes make it clear that the mayor
was livid because the instructions he had sent for them to cease their activity and his threat of legal action had been ignored, and he did not like
being questioned or challenged.) "We were not expected to fight back.
The mayor thought we would just sit back, be quiet and docile and say
'Yes, sir'," said Jackie. But more fuel was added to the petitioners' anger
when their own band manager publicly ridiculed them by commenting
to the mayor that they were "just the little people doing this. They don't
mean anything!"

Mazie recalled what happened next:

> Well, then the cops showed up. They came over and asked, "Who's doing this road block?"
>
> I said, "I am. I want a light for my kids or I'm not letting them go back to school. I don't want them to have an education and die on the way to doing it."
>
> And Jackie Gonzales and Earl Newman came over to hear what was going on, and Earl said, "Yup, we're road-blocking."
>
> And the cop said, "You can't do that. It's not legal. We're giving you warrants and you have to appear in court."
>
> "Fine," we said. "We'll go to court, but we're doing this road block today."

North Vancouver's city councillors were not pleased by the actions of these Squamish Nation picketers, and even more displeased when Chief Philip Joe — who had become a late convert to the cause — came before the council with a list of improvements that the band wanted — sidewalks, flashing signal lights at Forbes, Mission and Mahon, reduced speed limits and tougher radar patrols at peak traffic times. They turned him down and told him that the 1976 city budget would include changes to improve the flow of traffic through that corridor, such as widening Third to four lanes and installing a central divider. However, more police radar patrols at peak times would not be possible because of traffic congestion at that time of day. In the meantime, the picketing group was to cease their activities or action would be taken against them.

As the "improvements" city council described were focussed primarily on improving traffic flow and not on safety for the Squamish people, the group continued with its information picketing, and a very angry mayor contacted the city's lawyers, the long-established Vancouver firm of Bull, Housser & Tupper, instructing them to obtain an interlocutory injunction against Jackie, Mazie, Earl and Percy. Plainclothes police officers came down to Third Street and took photos of the picketers while uniformed police took down names. "We were treated like terrorists as if we were a threat to the City," said Jackie.

Meanwhile, support for the Third Street picketers had been arriving in the city's offices. In a letter dated November 4, 1975, N.A. Fulton, supervisor of services for School District 44, North Vancouver, noted that, as he had requested earlier, a crossing guard would be placed on Third Street at Mission on a temporary basis, but he pointed out that this was not a solution to the traffic safety conditions in the vicinity:

> Placement of an adult guard will improve safety during school opening, noon and dismissal times on school days but does not improve safety at other periods of time. Visibility and the lack of separation of vehicular and pedestrian traffic by sidewalks are significant problems in this area.

The Queen Mary Community Association sent a scathing letter to the mayor and council declaring their full support of the picketers' actions and their requests for safety measures. A letter also came from the Queen Mary Community Council, and even the North Vancouver Communist Party sent a letter to the mayor and council expressing their support for the picketers.

However, despite this show of support, the hearing for an injunction in the traffic light debacle was quickly moved to the Supreme Court of British Columbia, presided over by the Honourable Mr. Justice John C. Bouck. On October 27, prior to the actual hearings, the court viewed evidence in the form of the photographs of the picketers and heard affidavits from three representatives of the City of North Vancouver. The war hero and former Member of Parliament Charles Cecil Merritt, QC, represented the Corporation of the City of North Vancouver. The band council, which was required to provide legal counsel for all band members, appointed Harry A. Slade, the band's own lawyer, to represent Jackie, Mazie, Earl and Percy at the hearing on October 29 and 30.

The four defendants, however, were uneasy having the band council's lawyer represent them as they felt it was his role to represent the council but not the people, which to them was an important distinction. As a result, prior to the beginning of the court proceedings they made it clear to Slade: "You represent us, you speak for us." But after the first session Jackie and Mazie were not pleased with his demeanor in the courtroom, and Jackie confronted him in the elevator and asked if he had something wrong with his voice as he spoke so quietly, *too* quietly.

"Can't you speak up for us?" she demanded. "The judge almost fell out of his chair trying to hear what you were saying."

Slade, surprised by the assertiveness of the women, turned red and replied, "If you don't want me to represent you …"

He was cut off by a frustrated Jackie. "We kind of have no choice. You were appointed our lawyer, so you are it. Just make sure you do a good job. We are not going to jail and that is the bottom line."

The hearing concluded on October 30 with the court granting an injunction to the City of North Vancouver against Jackie, Mazie, Earl and Percy plus "any other person or persons whose identity was unknown." Pending trial, they were restrained from blocking or obstructing Third Street or any other highway within the City of North Vancouver. The document concluded with a *nota bene* on the last page, which warned that if they ignored the order they would be liable to a "process of execution" for the purpose of compelling them to obey.

Their second court appearance followed just a few days later, and they arrived to find a full courtroom, half of them people from the reserve who had come to show their support. Mazie was not at all intimidated by the court setting, and as she knew how to turn her illiteracy into a positive tool when she needed to, before the proceedings had even begun, she stood up and announced to the judge:

> Excuse me, before we go into serious talking about what's happening here, I'd like to tell you I don't have any education, and I don't know how to read. When I get up on the stand, you might say some big words that I'm not gonna understand. You may have to tell me ten, twenty different times, different ways to say it. When I understand, then I'll answer you.

This session in court was very short. The judge sided with the parents and protestors, not the City of North Vancouver. According to Mazie:

> The judge just looked at everybody and said, "This is just ridiculous! Get these people out of here and give them that light! Why waste my time? This woman has been fighting so hard to keep her kids alive. You guys give them that light."

And the case was dismissed. However, the court's refusal to provide a resolution to the dispute moved its settlement back into the hands of the City and the Squamish Band, and they would finally have to make a serious attempt to come to some agreement. There was one problem: the injunction was still in place, and there would obviously be no progress while it existed. At 3:00 p.m. on November 13 an informal meeting was held in the council chamber of North Vancouver's city hall. In attendance were the members of the city council and the Squamish Band council plus Mazie Baker, Jackie Gonzales, Earl Newman and Percy Paull. When the four defendants announced at the beginning of the meeting that they wanted the injunction lifted, Mayor Reid responded that he was prepared to lift it provided they gave assurance that their demonstrations would not be resumed. He then outlined the city's plans for Third Street, and this was followed by discussions that covered the pros and cons for the requested light, the widening of the road and the possibility of increased radar. However, the city engineer countered every suggestion for implementing change that was put forward by the city council members and the Squamish Band with numerous reasons why they would not be feasible. Finally Alderman Braithwaite, who was obviously in agreement with the band's safety requests, asked the engineer, "If lights have to go in at Third and Forbes, why could they not be installed without widening the road?" The reply was that it would be physically possible to install the lights but, because of the amount of traffic on Third Street, it would be very difficult and would result in immense public pressure to remove them. He added that a pedestrian-activated light, rather than a full stop light, would create the same problem.

Mazie and Jackie listened to all of this in disbelief. The heavy traffic speeding along Third Street was the reason they had put up their blockade in first place, and here that same traffic was being used as a reason for *not* doing anything to resolve the problem because the public would not approve. What was the difference, they wondered, between the people of the reserve and this "public" they were talking about? Were they not part of the public, too? Was it not their children who were being endangered? What would have happened if the City's public had put up a blockade?

At the end of the meeting the mayor asked that the Squamish Band Council give assurance in the form of a resolution or their word as gentlemen that demonstrations would cease. Dave Jacobs, representing the band council, replied that they had discussed this and advised the people against whom the injunction was made not to appeal it and not to demonstrate again until the councils of the band and the city had met to see what could be done about Third Street safety. This, he said, had not been a band council resolution, but the people had agreed to it. The meeting adjourned with no real decisions being made as this was not the forum for such actions; an official city council meeting would be needed to move forward to some kind of agreement on both the road improvements and the injunction.

That meeting was set for November 17, but when the city's lawyers, Bull, Housser & Tupper, were informed prior to the meeting that the council was considering lifting the injunction, they advised against it. Despite this advice, at the meeting the council did pass a motion that action be taken to alleviate the traffic problems on Third Street through the Mission Indian Reserve area. Radar patrols were to be increased adjacent to Mission and Delbrook streets, 30-mph signs were to be erected, signage was to be posted warning motorists of the two-lane traffic ahead, a traffic light at Third and Ridgeway was to be installed, a crossing guard placed on duty at Third and Mission Road, and concrete abutments were to be positioned. This was not a complete list of the Squamish band's requirements, but a further meeting between the council and the band was to be held as soon as council received the results of their application to the provincial government for a grant under the Community Disparity Fund for further improvements to Third Street. Finally a motion was made and passed to lift the injunction.

Two days later a letter was sent from city council to Chief Philip Joe informing him and the band council of their decisions, and also notifying them that the traffic light at Third and Ridgeway was now functioning and there was a crossing guard at Mission Road. Another letter, dated December 31, informed them that the city council had received $100,000 from the Community Disparity Fund for the reconstruction of Third Street between Bewicke and Forbes avenues. The letter also stated that Council wished to meet with the Squamish Band Council early in 1976 to discuss the improvements and the amount of widening to be done on Third Street.

This was progress indeed! In the space of two and one-half months the determined group of activists had picketed and forced the Squamish Band Council to become involved, despite their original reluctance. They had put in two court appearances — one placing an injunction against the four leaders of the insurrection, the second resulting in the judge admonishing the city's representatives and telling them not to waste court time — attended special meetings between the city council and band council, seen the city capitulate to demands for road improvements and lift the injunction, and finally seen the city invite the band council to join in planning the road improvements on Third Street.

Mazie's first flight into city politics had been a roller coaster, but she remained undaunted and tenacious. She and the determined Jackie Gonzales had become a joint force to be reckoned with, and their success flashed in front of them every day in the form of the traffic light at Mission Road.

In the mid-1980s Mazie Baker had occasion to fly into attack mode against the band council again.

> I was at a council meeting when they said they were going to build a road right beside the cemetery where Mum and Dad are buried. And I said, "What is this?"
>
> And they said, "Oh, we're going to build a road to go right through to the Sea Bus."
>
> "No, you're not," I said. "People are going to be throwing garbage out into the cemetery." And I said, "Do you think that I want to be stuck in there between two traffics? So I can't get out on the bottom road and I can't get out on Third? You gotta be nuts! There is no way I'm letting you do that."

> There were these guys in suits there — six of them all dressed up — and they said they would give [the band] a lot of money for permission to put that road through. "Nope, I'm tired of it," I told them. "I'm tired of people pushing me around and stepping all over me and slapping me in the face to give them more of my land." There was no way I was letting them get away with that.

Mazie's friend Jackie Gonzalez also became involved in this "lower road issue," and the two of them worked together to find out what was behind it. Mazie talked to people while Jackie did the document research, digging to find the background information on the proposal. "We were digging into files and records and causing so much controversy," said Jackie. "We didn't think that we were making a difference, but we did what we thought we needed to do." She discovered that the road was actually intended to go past the Seabus terminal and all the way to Deep Cove with a future crossing to Ioco on the other side of Indian Arm. This latter part of the project would involve going through land belonging to the Tsleil-Waututh Nation (People of the Inlet), which runs along Burrard Inlet. Even more importantly, they discovered that the proposal also included relocating people from the Mission Reserve to a new "mountain community." To put it mildly, this did not go over well. Squamish Nation people leaving their traditional lands by the water to live up the mountain was not going to happen.

While Mazie and Jackie did their research, the band council delayed making a decision on the road plans, and though there must have been other factors influencing the delay of which Mazie and Jackie were unaware, the two women plus their supporters on the reserve knew that they carried a lot of weight in the band's final decision to abort the planned road. "And that was the end of that," said Mazie. "The road never went through."

Mazie's experiences of negotiating and challenging such issues as school attendance with teachers, fighting the band council for a school bus and road bumps, battling both city and band for street lights and stopping an unwanted road through band lands had provided excellent training for what lay ahead. Her training flights were over.

9

Mazie and Alvie Baker had celebrated their twenty-fifth wedding anniversary with friends in 1976. Mazie recalled:

> One of them said, "Come on, Baker, make a speech!" Well, Alvie wasn't someone who liked to make speeches, you know, but he stood up and said, "I would like to tell May — that was his name for me — that for twenty-five years I have never had to wonder where she was. She would always be at home, have my meals on the table at 5:30 every night. I'd get home and my kids would be spotless and the house was clean. I could never find any woman like you, May — ever. I really appreciate what you do for me and our kids." Those were loving words to my ears. Then they asked me to make a speech, and I said, "Well, I can't top that, so whatever he said goes for me too. I could never find a father like him for our kids." And mind you, I wasn't drinking, even if it was our twenty-fifth anniversary! It was a great party and we laughed about going on for our fiftieth.

This was not to be. One day in 1988 Alvie Baker, who was then 58, was operating a crane on a freighter docked at LynnTerm in North Vancouver. Mazie remembered that day so clearly:

> He was way up on top of this ship, and I guess he didn't realize he'd had a stroke. He tried to holler down to the

worker below, but he couldn't talk so there was no way anybody knew he had a stroke way up there. He finally came down, and all the guys that were working that day had left the ship and he was there by himself. He got off the ship, got in his van, and he said it wouldn't start. Then he got to the phone booth to phone me, but he couldn't talk! So he went back to his van, and this time it started and he drove all the way home — about a ten-minute drive.

I was sewing my granddaughter Fail's regalia for the powwow. He comes in — usually he never came in — and he sits beside me and watches what I'm doing. "What's the matter?" I said. He just looked at me — he never said nothing, so I just kept on sewing, and I said, "What's the matter?" again. And he tried to talk to me, but he was just going "Bu-bu-bu bu-bu-bu …" He used to tease me like that when he had a few beers. And I said, "Don't be silly now. What is the matter?" And he just kept going, "Bu-bu-bu …" I said, "Is there something wrong with you?" And he nodded his head yeah. I said, "Do you want to go to the hospital?" And he nodded his head yeah. So I phoned my eldest son. I said, "There's something wrong with your father. I need you to come down and we will take him up to the Emergency."

The doctor at the Emergency said, "You're lucky you brought him in. He's had a stroke. We're going to keep him for a couple of days and see what's going on." And the next day I went up there, and he's had another stroke. But this time it took half of his right side. He could move his arm, but he couldn't move his legs and he couldn't talk. He couldn't swallow. And the doctors said he was going to be a vegetable. And my kids were standing outside the door crying. "We're not going to let Dad be a vegetable," they said. So he was in hospital for months.

One day my daughters and me happened to go up to the hospital and he was sitting in a chair like a baby's high chair, leaning way over the tray. And I said, "What's the matter with you? Are you tired?" And he sort of nodded, so I told Tammie, "Go get the nurses and ask them if they could put him back to bed." So she went down and found the nurse and said, "My mum would like you to put my father back in his bed." And we waited and waited, and I sent Tammie down again, and the nurse was sitting on another patient's bed watching *The Young and the Restless*. So I went down there to ask her, and she said, "Oh for God's sake, I just got him up ten minutes ago!" And I said, "I've been here half an hour waiting for you to come." She was a snooty nurse anyway, and she came into the room and me and Tammie were standing by his bed and she said, "Could you guys get out of here please! Go stand outside the door so I can get him into bed." So we stood outside the door watching her move him, and then she came and slammed the door on us. And I'm telling you everything just went black. I pushed the door open, and I said, "Get the hell out of here right now and don't ever touch my husband again!" I said, "Get! I will put him to bed!"

Before that happened, I gave up his private room 'cause there was a guy dying, and they needed the privacy for him. And now I said, "And I want that private room back right now, do you hear me? Do you understand what I'm saying?" And I was screaming at the top of my voice. I said, "Don't you ever come near my husband. You treat him like a slab of meat. Get out!" And she left and one of the doctors came by, and he gave the okay finger, and he said, "About time somebody told her off!" And I said, "Well, she better not come near my husband again. I want that private room right now!" Boy, five minutes and they had him in his private room.

I said, "See this door?" And that nurse said, "Yeah … " And I said, "Well, you're not allowed past that door, none of you. I will look after my husband." I had my kids write notes to say what [the nurses] could do and what they couldn't do. I said, "Before you come into this room, you knock on the door." I changed his bedding, I bathed him, gave him clean pajamas, put on clean sheets every morning, and I mopped his floor with their white towels 'cause I wouldn't let any of them into his room. I said, "Nobody treats my husband like that, least of all you." And the nurse, she came to the door and she knocked and said, "Mrs. Baker, if you like to mop his floor, there are mops down the hallway." And I thanked her.

Alvie wasn't able to talk or move his leg and foot, so my daughter Gloria would massage his foot and leg and move his leg and arm. We would sit him up, and I had to teach him how to swallow. I'd lift his chin up and put a drop of water on his tongue and he would have to swallow and finally he was eating soft stuff like Jell-O pudding. And then he wanted the *Province* paper. The nurse couldn't understand what he was saying 'cause he would just mumble. So I would say, "What do you want? You want the paper?" And he nodded his head "yes," so I went out and got the paper and gave it to him. He kept turning the pages, turning the pages not even looking at it. Then he came to a whole bunch of cars in the paper, and he pointed at one car. I said, "You're trying to tell me something about your car?" And he nodded his head. And I said, "You don't want your sons to drive your van?" No, that wasn't it. "Something to do with your van?" He nodded yeah. And I said, "The insurance is going to be up?" He started to smile 'cause that was what he was try-ing to tell me — to renew his insurance for him.

And this is how we went through everything. Then one day I said, "I'm not going to look at the papers any-more. I know you can talk and if you want to commu-nicate with me, you talk." Nope, he wasn't going to do that. So I went behind him where he couldn't see me and started telling him something, and I didn't know what I was talking about, and plain as day he said "What?" I said, "See! I told you you could talk!" And then he was laughing and crying at the same time. And I said, "So do you think you sound funny when you say words?" And he nodded. And I said, "Well, you know, when nobody is here, you talk to your kids. Call their names, each one of them, name them off." So he would do that, call his kids, and pretty soon he was talking.

Then one day the doctor come and said, "He's doing fine but he just still can't walk." So I was sitting there talking, and all of a sudden I noticed his sheet move down where his toes were. I said, "Your foot moved!" No, it didn't. I said, "Yes, it did!" Nope. So he was really ticklish on his feet, so I touched his feet and his knee come almost up to his chest. And I said, "See, I told you you could move it."

So this was going on for two months — over two months — and I still wouldn't let them come into the room. I would go up there to the hospital at seven o'clock in the morning, sponge him up, change his bedding, get him up, sit him in the chair for a while, sponge bath him, put him in a wheelchair and walk him around, come back and feed him. My kids would get up there about noon, so I could come home and a rest for about two or three hours and then I would go back up at six and stay with him until eleven. Every day the same routine because I would not let those nurses pull him down. And I said, "The only time you can come into that room is when I'm there." And then my doctor got wind of it. I went to see her 'cause I was so tired, and she'd been back east at some convention or other, and she said, "Mrs. Baker, what did you do to those nurses on the seventh floor? Everybody heard about you at the convention." And I said, "Well, I am not a person to fool around with. When I talk, I mean business."

When Alvie was strong enough to return home, the family team made sure there was always someone available to take him out for drives, visit

Mazie said, "I wanted a quiet husband, I was rowdy enough all by myself." They were happily married for forty-two years. Photo: Family collection, Keith Nahanee Jr.

friends and keep him engaged in his surroundings. Tammie said, "We set up a schedule — I would do two hours, Gloria would do two hours, Tia would do two. It worked well. We had good times with my dad." Alvie's team did a magnificent job of helping him regain most of his independence. But while his condition improved and he was able to talk and walk quite well — though still dragging his leg somewhat — he was never able to return to work after his stroke. And on June 10, 1993 — four years after his stroke — he had a heart attack and died. Mazie was shattered and it took some time for her to get back on her feet.

10

With Alvie gone, Mazie Baker needed to be involved in something meaningful to her, to her children and to her people. Ever since she was a child she had been fighting for what was fair, so now to her family's astonishment, she announced, "I have decided to get into politics." She was not entirely new to politics, of course. She had started attending the Squamish Nation's general meetings when she was in her twenties.

> When I first got married, Alvie's father, Willie Baker, used to always tell me and Alvie to get up there "and listen to the meetings." Same with my mum. She'd say, "You girls get up to those meetings because one day you're gonna be there fighting for whatever." And I thought, Nope! No way am I gonna be fighting for anything. Little did I know!
>
> My dad always told me, he said, "If you don't speak up for yourself, nobody else will." And I thank my dad for teaching me this. I used to say there is no way I'm getting up in front of a whole bunch of people and talk about what I need to have to talk about. But once you get that foot in the door, it is easy the rest of the way. And I do not bow to anybody or take a back seat to anybody. This is the kind of person I am. This is the kind of person that anyone has to deal with. The things I don't like, I get up and speak about them. I don't let it fester in me or disturb my life and my world with my kids. I cannot stand anybody that thinks they can come and boss me around.

The general meetings that Mazie attended were presided over by the chiefs and councillors elected according to the *Indian Act* of 1876, which had imposed a system that was completely contrary to the culture and traditions of the Coast Salish peoples, who had traditionally been governed by hereditary chiefs. However, after the sixteen villages had amalgamated to become the Squamish Nation in 1923, the people of the Nation had sidestepped the intentions of the *Indian Act* by electing their hereditary chiefs to their governing council. Mazie explained:

> The councillors, they would hand the job down to their sons. Like the father could say, "I'm retiring now, and I want you to take over my job," and he would hand it over to his oldest son or the youngest son. But when the older councillors started to die, the younger generation didn't want to be a councillor, so that's where it stopped. I don't think the young people went to the general meetings to find out what was really happening, you know. They thought that a council meeting was just where you went to blow off steam. And like, my husband was handed down a seat on the council, but he wouldn't be one. And my father-in-law kept telling me, "Come up to the general meeting and listen to what's going on because one day it is going to help you out." And I thought, what good is a council meeting? I don't need to know what's going on. But I went up there. My husband wouldn't go. And I listened to these chiefs and what they had to say.

Mazie discovered that she enjoyed the meetings and listening to the elders speak, especially the traditional chiefs:

> The old-timers—they were what I call real councillors and real chiefs. When Chief Moses Joseph spoke, everybody listened, you know? He'd say, "This is Squamish people. If they need something, you go there and see what they need." We never ever had to go there and fight to get our house renovated or to get food on our table or clothes on our kids. If they heard one of the guys was out of work, the chiefs would say, "I heard this guy is

not working. You go down and check and see if he needs help. Give him a voucher, and check his cupboards — if he needs food, give him a voucher. If he needs clothes for those kids, you give him a voucher." Now that was a real chief looking after his people.

At one of the meetings the Indian agent was there, and the chief said to the Indian Agent, "You do not hold a membership in this Reserve, so we would like you to leave. This meeting is for the Squamish people." So the Indian agent — his face was just red he was so mad — he got up and he left, and they passed a motion that nobody was allowed into any of our meetings unless they held a membership. After he left, then everyone started talking and saying what their problems were, and the chief and council said they would deal with them and they did.

They knew what was right and wrong for them and they always told us, "When we lease out land, we always put 50 percent of the money away and give the people 50 percent. This way we will never go broke." And that was fair with all the members. They were satisfied that 50 percent would be put away for education, for housing, for whatever we need. And 50 percent would go to the people — that was fine. And they believed in looking after their people. Not like today. The chiefs and council today they'll get up and say one thing and turn around and do another.

The federal government's law enforcing the election of chiefs and council members — one councillor for every hundred band members — gradually weakened the influence of the traditional chiefs. Mazie was never impressed with this system, and in her later years she had little time for most of the elected chiefs and councillors. She said:

There are too many chiefs and not enough Indians in our land today — I call them store-bought chiefs. They only think of themselves, nobody else. I'm sorry to say I do not call them chiefs. I call them by their given names.

> The only one that calls them chief is the white man. If
> they had to earn a feather from me, they would be lucky if
> they got a crow feather and that's insulting the crow! Ev-
> ery time you turn around they are buying blankets to give
> away to become a chief. Now if you are a real chief, you
> should act like a chief, not stand on the hill and dominate
> your people. When they can prove to me they are looking
> after their people, then one day I may call them chief.

Unfortunately for the Squamish Nation's chiefs and councillors, Mazie had now become a very powerful force on the reserve. While as a
youngster she had garnered a reputation for being feisty and outspoken
within the reserve, as an adult she had become trusted and respected as
the matriarch she had become. But the band councillors were not always
delighted to see her flying into the band offices or showing up at council
meetings. Her appearance was a sure indicator that an issue was brewing
and feathers would likely be flying. Mazie remembered:

> I know when I first started, I didn't think I could get up
> and talk in front of all the people and chiefs and council.
> But I would talk to myself and say, "Nope, these are my
> people and my relatives, and I have the right to say what I
> want when I go to general meetings." Then I started get-
> ting up and talking. I would tell them what I liked and
> what I didn't like about the things they were doing, and
> why. I really learned a lot and soon I was really comfort-
> able going to those meetings and speaking. When I knew
> an important thing was on the agenda, I would go, and
> when I walked in and they looked up and saw me, some
> of them would just put their heads down on the table and
> groan! Now what does that tell you? At times like that I
> always smile and remember my mom telling me about
> the times she would go over to the Indian agent's office,
> and he would say, "Well, Sarah, what have we done now?"
> Yeah, I'm my mother's daughter, a fighter, and proud of it.

Her reputation as a fighter for her family and her people resulted in others on the reserve going to her when they had problems with the council.

Jakatar, a Mi'Kmaq from Stephenville Crossing, Newfoundland, and family friend, was witness to many occasions when people came to her to explain things to them or to ask her to speak for them at the meetings. He said:

> She was so well respected in the community people would come to her for counsel on a regular basis. She would sit at her dining room table and people would come and go. They all wanted advice on what was going on in the neighbourhood. Just watching her and the way she dealt with people impressed me. She held her head up high with dignity and respect for others. She told things how they were. It was not always pleasant. She was strong, steadfast and would not bend from that resolute position. If that meant she had to look bad in somebody's eyes, so be it. She didn't always end up impressing people and making new friends.

Mazie was not prepared to do their fighting for them; instead she would coach them then go with them to the meeting. She said:

> They always come and say, "Auntie [Mazie was Auntie to everybody on the reserve] we need you to go to council and talk about this or that problem." So I sit and talk with them, then I say, "Now I want *you* to go to council and talk. I know it's not easy for a lot of people to get up and talk, but I would like you to talk, and if you start stumbling then that is when I will get up and help you. And if you cry when you are talking, that's okay. That's allowed. I would like you to try to stand on your own two feet. I will be there for you. I will stand beside you, but I would really like you to have your own power." Whatever I say, the people still tell me, "We need you at all the meetings 'cause you're not afraid to speak up." And I tell them, "I would like to be at all the meetings and fighting for you, but there are times I can't come and I would like you to learn to stand up and speak out for what you believe in. Nobody can shut you down in a general

meeting. *You have the right to speak.* That is what the chiefs
and council are there for — to listen to your problems."

It isn't easy for them. They are frightened something bad will
happen, or that they won't be able to open their mouths, or they
will look stupid or cry or not understand. I think we still got a
long way to go. What will they do when I'm gone? They gotta
learn to stand up for themselves when I'm not around.

Mazie was most concerned about the low turnout for general meetings
because it meant that only a very small percentage of the community was
deciding the important issues. However, she knew they were avoiding the
meetings because they did not know or understand what was going on.

Every time they had a general meeting there were only
about sixty people there. What can you do with sixty?
Something needed to be changed. We finally passed the
"75 percent of the whole population" motion at a meeting. Now nothing can go through without 75 percent of
the people's approval.

Then there was the band's practice of giving out the
distribution cheques next to the voting booths. Everyone wants to get their money so they turn up to get their
cheques and go in to the booths to vote. It was like, "Here
is your money, now come and vote." And that looks like
paying people to vote. They'd just got their cheques from
the band and they felt good. It influenced their votes, right?

Mazie had her own remedy for this. She would have someone explain
the issue thoroughly to her, then she would stand near the voting booths
to meet the people as they came to vote and ask them, "Do you know
what you're voting for? Do you want this? If you don't, it's okay to vote
no. Just because you got your cheque today doesn't mean you have to
agree to something you don't want or don't understand." She would take
the time to explain to many of them what the vote was for, and inevitably
some would ask her to tell them whether to vote yes or no. Her answer
was always: "Now you know what it's about, you have to decide what's
best for you. I can't tell you how to vote."

Accountability was a crucial component in her dealings with others, especially youth. Typical of her determination to instill accountability into the young was the summer day in 2008 when a young male relative dropped by to talk to her about the trouble he got into when he was drunk. She listened patiently while he told her that he really wanted to quit and be healthy, but he had no money to go to the rehab program on Vancouver Island. She was familiar with this program as two of her daughters were graduates and had been clean and sober for many years. Despite this, she was not willing to just hand over money to help him. She told him, "Ya gotta be serious about getting sober, not just talk about it and complain." They talked for a long time about accountability. She said, "It's tough getting sober. You gotta believe you are a worthwhile person." At that point the young man broke into tears. Unfazed, she continued, "I will be there for you, but you gotta tell me you are listening to my words, and be responsible for your actions. No actions, no support. I'm not gonna talk to you or help you if you aren't prepared to do the work." This was tough love. He left, saying he would think about everything she had told him and come back later.

Each task she took on eventually brought about change, though not always enough for her to sit back, relax and feel her work was finished. Her outspoken methods and sheer determination sometimes caused friction so that she was not the most popular person with some members of the band council. She shed no tears over this, but moved on to the next thing that she felt had to be aired and "fixed."

11

It is a common misconception that all Indian reserve lands in Canada are held in common by all members of the reserve. While it is true that *some* reserve land is held communally, the federal government long ago decided that assigning individual property ownership on reserves would hasten the integration of the Aboriginal population into the white man's way of life and economy. So in time Indian Affairs invented four types of individual property rights regimes on reserves, though today by far the most common is the certificate of possession (CP) system, which in 1951 replaced an earlier system called location tickets. A CP is the evidence of an individual band member's lawful possession of a particular tract of reserve land for the purpose of building a house or a business or exploiting the land's resources, such as timber or minerals, or farming it. For an individual to acquire a CP to a specific piece of land, usually one on which his family has lived or farmed for generations, the applicant petitions the band council for ownership, the council allots the land to the applicant, and the minister of Indian Affairs approves the allotment.

However, holding a CP for a piece of reserve land is not the same as private property ownership off-reserve. In Canadian law there are two main types of private property ownership: estate in fee simple and a life estate in the land. Fee simple ownership means the individual has the absolute and exclusive use of the land and has the right to sell it or will it to someone else. Life estate ownership means the individual owns the land only as long as he lives; he cannot exploit its natural resources and he can neither sell it nor will it to anyone else. The *Indian Act* does not specify either of these types of ownership for CP owners. Instead, ownership lies somewhere in the no man's land between the two: the individual has lawful possession and may lease the land out to either a member of the band or a non-member. He may divide the land among his children or may transfer part of his interest in the land to another member of the band such as a spouse, so that they hold the CP as tenants in common or joint tenants. However, such arrangements are only legal if the minister approves. No sales or transfers can be made to persons who are not members of that band, and no legal provision has been made for the division of property in the case of divorce. These last two issues have resulted in long-running battles between Native communities and their band councils as well as numerous court cases.

Mazie Baker was very proud of her certificates of possession for six lots on the Stawamus reserve in Squamish as well as two on the Mission reserve. She would laugh and say, "I am a land baroness!" But for Mazie, owning reserve property was not always free of problems. There were several occasions when she had to defend her own property rights as well as those of family members. Her first skirmish with the Squamish Band council over family property happened in the mid-1980s over a lot belonging to her young adopted brother, Roger, who was in jail and could not fight for it himself. The ensuing battle caused a major upheaval in the community. She recalled:

> I was at Bingo one night and someone comes up and says, "Mazie, you know they're building on your brother's lot?" And I said, "WHAT?" So the next day I went down, and yup, Roger's old house was torn down and there they were, halfway done with this new house. I told the guys working on it, "You guys better stop building on that 'cause it doesn't belong to you, you know—it belongs to my brother Roger." They just ignored me and kept building away. I went home and asked Gloria to write a letter for me, saying that I want them to stop building the house on my brother's lot. So I went down to where they were building. These young guys are all members of the Nation who were building there. And the foreman,

> he said, "What you got here, cous?" And I said, "Read
> it." And he said, "Okay, cous, this is terrible. We'll shut
> down right now and we'll come up to the band office
> and see what council is going to do about it." So all the
> workers got down from the roof and whatever, and we
> all marched up to the band office. Well, we got there
> and we passed the letter out to them, and the council
> wouldn't listen to me. They thought, okay we can run
> all over her.

The band council's refusal to hear Mazie out only served to make her angrier and more determined than ever.

> I went door to door all the way down to the Capilano
> reserve, bringing that letter to each home. We didn't have
> the Seymour reserve at the time. About fifty of us rushed
> into the council room, and I said, "I want you guys to
> stop building on my brother's lot, and I'm not going to
> tell you again." And Joe Mathias, he was chief at that
> time, and he said, "We're not stopping this meeting for
> anyone. We're going on with our meeting." Then all the
> people that were there shouted, "No! Stop the meeting!
> We need to talk to you." And he just ignored all of us.
>
> So we started calling a general meeting. And you
> wouldn't believe the people that showed up for these
> meetings. They were so fed up with the way they were
> running our band. We had … I don't know … maybe
> ninety people that showed up, and they were really rip-
> ping down that council and chiefs.

In the end the council brought an end to the clamouring voices by announcing that they needed to have "a proper meeting without everyone arguing." Mazie, however, was still fired up and not ready to quit yet.

> And I said, "How can you guys argue about what's not
> yours? This lot, this land belongs to my brother. And why
> are you still building on it when you know that building
> should have been stopped long ago?" And Mathias said,

"No, we're not stopping for anybody. You guys go ahead and keep building that house." And I said, "No, you're not." And I told them, "It belongs to my brother, so I want you to realize I'm not going away. I'm going to fight you right through to the end." So we went to war and that's when everything broke loose.

Timing is everything. A few days later Mazie happened to be at the band office when she overheard someone say, "I've got Roger's signature here on this paper stating we can have his lot." Mazie recognized it as the voice of the daughter-in-law of the council's chairman.

As she walked by the open door, I snatched the paper out of her hand, and I said, "You are not gonna use that." She said, "Why not?" I was mad! I had some people with me and I asked them to read the paper for me. They told me that she had gone to the jail and Roger had signed it, but there were no witnesses that he had signed it. When I told her that, she just said, "Well, I was bringing it down for Gloria to sign." I knew Gloria wouldn't touch that paper with a ten-foot pole 'cause she hadn't seen Roger sign it. That paper would have given my brother's property to the son of the chairman of the council. They were all in it together — he was chair, his wife worked in the housing department and his daughter-in-law was the secretary for the chiefs and council meetings. They were building that new house on Roger's property for the chairman's son!

Mazie attended yet another chiefs and council meeting and asked them how come the rest of the community had to follow rules and regulations, but the chairman, his wife and his daughter-in-law did not. Her questions went unanswered, and they wouldn't agree to do anything about their conduct. But it happened that Jo-Ann Nahanee had attended one of the general meetings at the band office and she could see that the chiefs and council were not going to do anything about Roger's lot. She recounted:

What I heard was way out of line for the way things
should be. I wanted to help in some way, and then I
found out that no one had typed up the minutes of the
meeting. So I stepped up and said I would type them over
the long weekend. As I typed, I just became more and
more shocked at what had been done. I took the minutes
over to Mazie, and she was really grateful to have them.
I asked her if there was anything else I could help with.

Meanwhile, Mazie had teamed up with her friend Jackie Gonzales, who immersed herself in researching the band's land records and
checking the Department of Indian Affairs' records and maps, pulling
together a damning collection of evidence. Jackie was stunned by what
she uncovered:

I was really innocent then. I thought everybody was on
the up and up. I never even suspected the corruption
that was going on. I discovered that property where St.
Thomas Aquinas is now had been under an agreement
that the property was supposed to come back to us as it
was originally Squamish Nation land. It never has. All
kinds of other things started coming out. But we were
called liars when we started giving out information about
that land, even though we had the documents. I spent a
lot of time digging through old records and discovered
that Mazie's case was not the only one. We went over to
Indian Affairs and got a printout of all the actual registries and then looked up the land surveys. Different lines
had been drawn over each other so the actual truth could
not be seen in the paperwork shuffle. Council was furious, and they went to the registries in town and told them
not to allow us access to the information. It's a long time
ago now but that's how it was at that time.

Mazie now mustered her troops, and Jackie Gonzales, Harriet Nahanee, Bill Williams, Gibby Jacob and Wilma Guss all helped her get ready
for the battle ahead. Mazie recalled:

Each time we had a meeting, the people would tell their friends what was going on, and pretty soon there was too many people to meet in the band office, so we went up to Hamilton School, just above Sears. And they had a count of heads, and there was 479 band members at this meeting, and that was the biggest meeting we ever had because I think people realized what I was doing was probably something that nobody had done before. Nobody ever stood up to the chiefs and council. And I said, "Well, we have to put a stop to it now or it's going to go on and on." And I told them, "I'm one that doesn't sit back and take whatever anybody wants to dish out to me."

And Jackie added:

We were prepared for a huge general meeting; we did all the research, the paperwork, showing the history, and we made copies of all the minutes of previous meetings and copies of the document Roger had been asked to sign, ready to share with everyone. We photocopied and stapled until our hands almost fell off. We had to have the meeting in the gym because 479 people showed up. It was a full house. This meeting was the first time that the people had heard all the information and actually seen the proof that council had tried to misconstrue that information, saying we were making assumptions and making things up.

The people were angry, and it was clear that they were solidly behind Mazie and her crew. They did not like what they were hearing about the underhanded business that had been going on. Mazie remembered:

The people were so angry with the seven councillors involved they said, "We don't want you representing us anymore. We will not let you sit on the council anymore. You're off, you're gone!" They wouldn't fire Joe Mathias because he was the chief, and I said, "Well, that's up to you. You call him your chief, but I'll never call him my chief. I'm sorry but that's just how I feel. I think a chief should be fighting with the people, not against them. But if this is what you guys want, that's up to you. Always remember this, if you leave a rotten apple in the barrel, it will rot the rest of them, you know?"

The ones who worked in the band office were fired because of what they did, but they paid them, the three of them, $99,000 — that's $33,000 each. And I said, "You think that's making it right? You know, for what they did? You fire them and then you go and pay them off?" I couldn't understand that. That doesn't seem right to me.

While all this was going on, Jackie's husband received death threats, her dog was shot, and her kids were threatened. And when Mazie left a meeting at the band offices to go to the bathroom, she was confronted by a woman who said she was going to beat the hell out of her.

I told her, "You go right ahead and try it." Her dad heard us arguing and he came out to see what was going on. I said, "You better keep your daughter away from me! If not, I'm phoning the police and she will be gone 'cause I'm gonna charge her with threatening me." He told her to get back in the meeting, but before he left, I told him, "I respect you while I am in a meeting. I want the same respect from you in a meeting. My kids never go and threaten you or your kids, and I don't want your kids threatening me or any of my kids. I will not stand for *anyone* threatening me." After that, they laid off.

In the end Roger did not get his lot back. Instead, he was given a lot with a brand new house on it on the Seymour reserve. Maisie was not mollified: "The exchange of lot and house gave him a nice house, but the point was that they should not have done what they did to start with."

In 1996 Jackie Gonzales resigned from her position with the band as she felt that if she stayed she was part of the corruption. As well, the threats to her family were nerve-wracking, and as they didn't feel safe in their own community anymore, they moved to the US. After her departure, Mazie's eldest son, Bucky, was the lone person working with the band's youth as all the other programs had disappeared. Jackie was desperately needed, and in 2003 she returned at the request of the band to redevelop the youth programs.

12

Mazie had been very surprised to discover, after Alvie died in 1993, that she owned property on the Stawamus reserve:

When Alvie was so sick I went over to the Department of Indian Affairs (DIA) to get the papers they had signed for me giving me power of attorney for him. I just didn't want the band council digging into my affairs, you know. A lady there called Evelyn who helped me told me this was a good thing I was doing 'cause it meant that I would get the will directly, and it would not go to the band council. It was only a couple of weeks later that Alvie died — June 10, 1993 — and I had to go over to DIA again, now that I was executor of his will. The lady said, "Everything he owns is going in your name. This means you are also responsible for paying any outstanding bills he may have." I was okay with that. I knew what had to be paid anyway. Well, was I surprised, though, when she brought out this big file! "This belonged to your husband," she said, "but he never came to see what it was all about." Then I got to find out about all the land he owned. I never knew anything about it. I was speechless, and that doesn't happen very often, now does it?

I found out that when my father-in-law, William Baker, made out his will, he named all his sons — five with his first wife and three with his second wife, Margaret, my mother-in-law — and his one daughter. But he left all his property — all six lots at Stawamus — to Alvie, his youngest son. It seems all the other sons had property up there at Stawamus already. He also left Alvie in charge of looking after the house next door to us here on the Mission Reserve. It was to be for Alvie's mum, Margaret, after his dad passed away. After Margaret's day it was to go to Ronnie, a grandson they adopted when he was a baby. Well, Alvie was supposed to look after that too, but I don't think he even knew about the will because he never mentioned it to me. He did know the house was to go to Ronnie, though.

When she inherited the six certificates of possession from her husband in 1993, Mazie knew she would have to understand the system thoroughly. She was not going to allow the Baker land to be taken from her and her family to become a development for someone else's financial gain. She prepared for her fight by drawing on everything she had learned during the fight to save Roger's lot in the mid-1980s and by making sure she thoroughly understood the rights her CPs gave her. For this she turned to her niece, Wendy Lockhart, who knew how to navigate her way through complicated government documents.

Not long after Mazie inherited the property on the Stawamus reserve, she had drafted a will allocating the lots to her family members and placed the will in her file at the Land Trust in the band office for safekeeping. Later she was surprised to receive a letter from the band council telling her that three people had applied to the council for ownership of her land in Stawamus. One of them had requested a specific lot and identified it as the one her son Alvie wanted. This information about the allocation of lots was supposedly private, and the only way anyone would have known which lot Alvie was to inherit was by reading Mazie's will in her private file at the Land Trust.

I went down to the band offices to ask how somebody would know information from my private file. They had no idea how it could have happened. Nobody was supposed to be able to read our files. Well, that was it for me! I wasn't gonna leave anything there anymore. So I told them from now on I'm strictly gonna deal with the DIA.

But based on her past experiences with the band council, she also knew that she had to move quickly to establish her ownership:

Council meetings were on the third Wednesday of the month, and band members wanting to bring something before council had to get their names on the agenda, so I headed down to the band office and put my name down. I was ready and I had all my papers with me. I started off saying, "I would like to know who owns this land." Then I handed over all my papers to the council to read. It didn't take long for Bill Williams to say, "It's yours, Mazie. No argument. All the proof is here." Well, that was good, but I wanted it actually written down as proof that I owned this land and nobody else is entitled to it but me. I wanted a signed paper in my hands ... just in case, you know. So they agreed to that. Then I told them I wanted them to write to those three who applied for my land and tell them they have no claim to it. They agreed to that too. I left feeling like that was it — there would be no more hassles around my property.

It could have turned out very differently. The councillors had not known that Mazie had those certificates of possession in her private file at the Land Trust, nor did they have a copy of Alvie's will. They could have granted the requests for those Stawamus lots, although had they done so, there is no doubt they would have had a major fight on their hands. Fortunately Mazie had heard about the claims in time to go to the council with her proof of ownership. As a result, this "fight" over her certificates was almost a non-event. However, her wish that there would be no more hassles around her property would soon prove to be only that — a wish, one that was not to be granted.

In accordance with the wishes of William Baker, Mazie's father-in-law, the house on the Mission Reserve beside the one where Mazie and

Alvie had brought up their nine children was to pass to Margaret, Alvie's mother, and after her death to Ronnie, the grandson that William and Margaret had adopted and raised. After Ronnie's death, ownership passed to Alvie, and in due course Alvie left it to Mazie. At that point there was an unexpected development: Ronnie's birth mother re-appeared to lay claim to the house. Frowning as she recalled the events that followed, Mazie said:

> I tell you this owning of property is a lot of work if you want to keep it. It was easier in the old days when everything belonged to the Creator and we were to take care of it and respect everything in it and on it. People get so cranky!

Recalling how Ronnie's adoption had come about and why it had been so important to the senior Bakers that he was provided for, Mazie continued:

> I remember babysitting Ronnie down at my sister's place. I wasn't even married to Alvie then, and this little guy had his hands tied to the cot — I found out later it was because he had eczema — but he was soaking wet, and I was scared [to change him] because I didn't know what [disease] he had. Alvie happened to come down and he knew Ronnie, so he went to his parents' house and told them what state he was in. They came over and took him home and looked after him, but his mom was gone for days and finally abandoned him, leaving him with Alvie's mom and dad. They decided they would keep him safe by adopting him and went before council and explained that Ronnie's mom had never come back to get him, and that they wanted to adopt him. The band council helped them with the adoption and Ronnie grew up with my in-laws and was part of their family. Which is why William made sure in his will that he would be looked after. Ronnie was always sickly, though — he suffered real bad from asthma. Once when I was babysitting him, he had a real

bad attack and was struggling to breathe, and I thought he was gonna die. Alvie's parents were Shaker and didn't believe in hospitals, so I didn't know what I should do. I told Alvie he *had* to do something. The kid couldn't just lie there; he needed help. Well, Alvie somehow managed to get them to take Ronnie to the hospital — I have no idea how he managed to persuade them. They rushed him to Lions Gate Hospital and they put him in a tent so he could breathe. Boy, I tell you, I was relieved. I'd been sure he was gonna die while I stood watching, helpless. He lived until he was 40 or so, which was amazing really 'cause he was always so weak, poor kid.

The reappearance of Ronnie's mother after all those years, claiming she owned the house, did not go over well with Mazie. The woman announced that since it had belonged to her son, it was now hers, and she was moving in. Mazie recalled:

I was so mad. She had never once come to see him in all those years! She hadn't seen him since he was a baby, but she came down from the North real fast after he died. I told her, "*I* have legal ownership." And she said, "I *will* get the house. I know how to get it." Well, that annoyed me no end, and I snapped at her, "No, you don't! It's under my name. I'll see you in court."

This fight was not going to be settled as easily as Mazie's earlier rounds of establishing ownership because she quickly discovered that someone from the band office had gone to the DIA's land registry as soon as Ronnie died and transferred the house and land into his mother's name. When Mazie went to the registry office, she was told there was nothing they could do because the band had already completed the transfer. At this point Mazie, drawing on her earlier experiences with the band council, decided to take the problem to the people. She called a general meeting.

I told council I had all the papers for the land, and I told them how the Bakers had adopted Ronnie because his mom had abandoned him. I reminded them that the council had helped with the adoption and that his mom had not once come to see him, only showing up after he died to grab his home. This property, I told them, belongs to the Bakers.

The council listened to Mazie's arguments, recognized her legal ownership of the house and returned it to the Bakers. But the outcome of this battle caused friction between the Bakers and the Nahanee families because Ronnie's mom was a Nahanee. And unfortunately, she was also the aunt of Keith Nahanee who was married to Gloria, Mazie's daughter. Recalling those days, Mazie said:

> I tell you, it was hard on all of us, but I had to make sure the wishes of William's and Alvie's wills were carried out. They were legal documents. If I hadn't been strong enough to stand up and fight for it, she would be living in that house today. It was a fair decision. There was a vote taken at the meeting and they decided it belonged to us. To stop her from going on to fight council, they gave her a lot up on Third Street that belonged to Jackie Gonzalez's husband, Frank, who agreed to let it go.

After the dust between the two families settled — which took quite a while — Mazie decided that owning these lots was a mixed blessing. Despite her earlier plans for their distribution among her own children, she decided to make new arrangements and called a meeting at her house for all of Alvie's brothers and their children.

> I told them I'm the only one fighting. Nobody's backing me up. I should not be on my own and going to council by myself to fight for family land. I said, "All of these lots belonged to Poppa Baker so each one of you can have a lot. You choose which one you want, and you are responsible for it." Lawrence's daughter Suzie was offered a lot, but she said she didn't want it if she had to go with me to council to fight for it. We then had to decide about Ronnie's house that had been returned to the family. I said I thought his house and lot should go to one of the

brothers, but I was not picking which brother — it was up to them to choose. Finally it was decided to give it to Billy, Thomas's son, because he had the most kids.

Lawrence was Poppa's eldest son, so he was upset that his dad had left all the lots to Alvie, the youngest son, and that now they were all in my name. Well, it wasn't something I had asked for. It was a while later when Lawrence, who was still upset, called me and told me I should have called a meeting! I told him I did call a meeting, and he was there, and Susie didn't want the lot. To settle this I called another meeting, and the family told him the same thing — there was a meeting, he was there, and Susie had said no to the lot. He just said, "Whatever." Susie still didn't want the lot, so I still have the empty lots up in Stawamus.

Despite these family meetings, the only lot that was allocated was Ronnie's; the others remained in Mazie's name because no one in the family wanted to move up to Stawamus; most of them had jobs and their own homes on the Mission Reserve or off-reserve. When asked what was going to happen to these Stawamus lots, Mazie's face lit up, and there was a twinkle in her eye:

> The band is interested in owning them and suggested they could make an exchange — those six lots for six lots on the Mission Reserve because they are short of lots up there. I told them if I was going to do a trade, I wanted homes on the Mission lots for my family *and* certificates of possession to go with them.

She chuckled and added:

> Well, we haven't even begun to meet on that yet. They did say we could talk about it. I told them they would be wheeling and dealing with the hardest person going.

13

First Nations housing is a topic frequently in the news right across Canada. It's a continuing story of shoddy buildings with leaking roofs, mold on the walls and poor insulation, of homes falling into dreadful disrepair and not being replaced or repaired, of massive housing shortages and unhealthy water supplies — all of them long-standing problems that are the result of poor federal and band policies. Native women, unfortunately, have been most seriously impacted by these policies, and the reasons for this date back to the *Indian Act* of 1876, which defined an Indian as any male person of Indian blood, any child of such a person and any woman — Indian or non-Indian — married to that male person. However, an Indian woman who married a non-Indian automatically lost her Indian status.

The act was amended in 1951 but it didn't improve the status of women. Section 11 continued the rule that any woman, Indian or non-Indian, who married a status Indian was automatically given status, while section 12(1b) reaffirmed that Indian women marrying non-Indians were not entitled to status. In addition, section 12 (1a)(iv), known as the "double mother" clause, provided that a person whose parents had married on or after September 4, 1951, and whose father was status Indian but whose mother and paternal grandmother had not been recognized as Indians before their marriages, could be registered as Indian at birth — but would lose that status on his or her twenty-first birthday. Being denied status meant that the person was also denied band membership, which meant losing the right to live on a reserve, vote for a band council, share in band income and own and/or inherit property on the reserve.

During the 1960s and 1970s women's groups organized opposition to these discriminatory clauses and formulated legal challenges, but these came to a dead-end in 1973 when the Supreme Court of Canada ruled that section 12(1b) did not violate the Canadian Bill of Rights. The one bright spot was a 1981 ruling by the United Nations Human Rights Committee that the terms of Canada's *Indian Act* ran counter to Article 27 of the International Covenant on Civil and Political Rights, which guarantees that persons belonging to minorities may enjoy their own culture. This finding, combined with continued pressure from women's organizations pushed the federal government toward further amendments to the act. At the same time, organizations such as the National Indian Brotherhood/Assembly of First Nations were arguing that it was not the place of government to decide band membership rights as they should be the prerogative of First Nations.

The federal government responded in 1985 with the compromise Bill C-31 that did away with the patrilineal definition of eligibility and replaced it with gender neutral rules, allowing the reinstatement of women who had lost status through marriage to non-Indians or due to the "double mother" clause. At the same time C-31 recognized the right of bands to determine their own membership, which meant that, although women could now regain their Indian status, they would not necessarily gain acceptance as band members. As required by the terms of Bill C-31, in 1987 the Squamish Nation released its first band membership code, which embodied the criteria to be used to grant or deny band membership to persons who had regained Indian status under the bill. The task of assessing those who applied for band membership was huge and required an incredible amount of genealogical research as each person had to be assessed separately, not as a family, before they could be accepted into the band. It was also a divisive system, and many people fell through the cracks as some band codes had been set up so that a mother might be granted status while her children or grandchildren were denied. Jackie Gonzales, who was involved in setting up a foundation to help those returning to their reserves, recalled:

> It was hard denying members by codes. There were people who belonged and had family here, but the codes

were set up in such a way that they would never be allowed back in. I had to tell John Cordecedo that he was not allowed to come back because of the codes. I tried explaining to him that it was a membership committee decision and told him about the codes. It was so hard. He was so upset, and it made no sense to him.

But those who were newly accepted or reinstated as band members faced a new problem: no homes. The well-intentioned Bill C-31 had inadvertently exacerbated the housing problems by suddenly increasing the population. According to a background document on Aboriginal Women and Housing that was prepared by the Native Women's Association of Canada for the Canada Aboriginal Peoples Roundtable of November 2004:

> Currently on reserves, a severe shortage of at least 8,500 units was documented in 2001 by the federal government, and in 2003 the Auditor General (AG) of Canada noted that figure as well as the need for renovations to 44% of existing housing stock on reserves. The AG also noted the projection that 4,500 new on-reserve households will be formed every year for the next ten years; however, current funding levels anticipate supporting the construction of only 2,600 homes per year ...
>
> The reinstatement of the registered Indian status of many Aboriginal women and their children who had lost registered Indian status prior to the changes to the Indian Act in 1985 ... resulted in a substantial increase in the demand for on-reserve housing through the late 1980s and since. Nearly twenty years later the waiting lists for housing on many reserves still reflect the inability to match supply with the demand for housing. The housing pressures created by the addition of reinstated members, 60% of whom were women, may have added to the chronic housing unit shortages noted above; however, poor policies and programs and a lack of adequate funding for band-owned housing and the availability of on-reserve home ownership loans are also implicated.

The reserves that have consistently garnered most of the national media coverage regarding this problem are primarily in Canada's eastern and northern regions, which inadvertently creates the impression that all is well in the west and especially in British Columbia. Not so. The reserves of the Squamish people, like most BC reserves, share many of the same problems: homes in a sad state of disrepair and a long list of people waiting for housing. Mazie's eldest daughter, Gloria, was one of those caught in the housing crunch. By the mid-1980s she and Keith Nahanee had been married and on the housing list for many years, and she was beginning to wonder when, if ever, they were going to get a house. Mazie remembered:

> She was living at my dad's [Moses Antone's] old house; it was cold and drafty for Riannon, her first baby, who was only two pounds when she was born. Gloria came here one day, just crying her eyes out. I asked what the matter was. "Well," she said, "I went to see when I was getting a house. I told them I was on the list." I knew fifteen new houses were being built, five on Mission, five on Cap[ilano] and five at Upper Squamish, and I already knew that out of those fifteen new houses one woman on the band council was getting six of them for her kids. I told Gloria, "Get your coat, stop crying, and we'll go back down there." We walked in and all the councillors were still sitting at the table. We went up to them and I asked, "What's happening with this housing list? How do you pick who's going to get a home?" That woman was sitting there. Her kids had only been married two years, and they were getting houses. She said, "Oh, we pick names out of a hat." So I said, "Well, yeah, but whose names do you put in the hat?" Eventually Gloria did get a house on her lot — she's just across the street from me. The housing list is still really long. In the '80s there were over eight hundred names on the list. It never seems to get any shorter.

Jackie Gonzales added:

> The 1980s were really bad, and that's when threats of violence came into play. Lots could only be in a man's name, females were excluded based on how the *Indian Act* was set up at that time. The old housing policy only had two categories for obtaining a house—pensioners and married couples. Divorced members were excluded, and there was no housing for single parents. Lots of homes became overcrowded; sometimes there was more than one family living in a house, and that created real stress and led to some abuse issues. Something had to change.

And Mazie continued:

> People have died while still on that list waiting for a house. It was never updated so you could be on the list for ten years or more. You almost have to get your kids names on the list while they're just little.

Advocating for a change in the Squamish Nation's housing policies became the next challenge for Mazie and Jackie, but they knew they needed everyone's involvement and input if the right kind of changes were to be made. Eventually they got all the families, single parents and grandparents together and went through the housing lists looking for ways to make them more equitable before they put their suggestions in front of the band council. It took two or three meetings to hammer it out, but a new housing policy was announced on October 10, 2001. (It was revised in April 2006.) Jackie said:

> It's still not everything we wanted. We wanted to do away with all the categories and have everyone, once they reached the age of majority, go on the list, so it would be equitable. It still isn't inclusive. There are no single-people homes being built, which is not fair to the high percentage of single people who still have no place to live. Some townhouses have been built, but no apartments or single-living units.

In recent years some new homes have been built under the Lions Gate Bridge, but they are not enough. According to the band, as of March 2011 there were about a thousand people on the housing list, and only three hundred vacant lots on the existing reserves.

According to evidence presented to the Senate Standing Committee on Aboriginal Peoples in May 1999, Nona Rose Lockhart was one of the women who was reinstated as a status Indian and a member of the Squamish band after Bill C-31 was passed in 1985. She had been born on the Mission Reserve in 1925, the only child of Mona and Henry "Hawkeye" Baker, an exceptional lacrosse goalie who played for Canada in the 1932 Olympics in Los Angeles. In 1966 he was inducted into the Canadian Lacrosse Hall of Fame, and in April 1999 he and two of his brothers, Ray and Dominic, were inducted posthumously into the BC Sports Hall of Fame as members of the famous North Shore Indians Lacrosse Team of 1936. (Henry Hawkeye Baker was a much older half-brother of Alvie Baker, Mazie's husband.)

In 1941 Nona requested assistance of the Department of Indian Affairs to attend high school in Vancouver; she had arranged to do housework for her board in the city but she needed money for her other expenses. Indian Affairs responded that:

> At this time the Department is not encouraging Indian girls to take higher academic training. However, we are prepared to supply her books if she attends high school, but it is not our intention to be responsible for any other expenses in connection with her education.[1]

As a result, Nona's education was cut short, and she was forced to go to work in unskilled jobs. In 1947 she married a non-Native and was automatically stripped of both her Native status and band membership. Her mother, Mona, died in 1967, and her famous father died the following year. In his last will and testament, which was approved by the Department of Indian Affairs, he left all his property to his only child as follows:

> I give all the property of which I die possessed as follows:
> Unto my daughter, Nona Rose Lockhart, all my assets,
> cash, my house and contents on Mission Indian Reserve

No. 1, and house on Stawamus Indian Reserve No. 24
and all of my property not herein before disposed of I
give to my daughter, Nona Rose Lockhart.[2]

However, because the Indian Act had stripped her of her status as
an Indian, Nona Lockhart was not permitted to inherit, or even live in,
either of the houses her father had willed to her. Instead, the Squamish
band council allowed a male band member and his non-native wife to live
in the house on the Mission reserve property and a male member of the
Sechelt Band to live in the Baker house on the Stawamus Reserve. Nona
received no compensation or rent for these properties. Although her status as an Indian and membership in the band were returned to her in
1985 under Bill C-31, according to evidence given to the Senate Standing
Committee in May 1999, the band refused to return her inheritance. In
January 1995 Nona had made a formal inheritance claim to her father's
property on Stawamus, but discovered that neither this property nor the
Mission Reserve property had been registered in her name. In December
1995 the band council dealt with her claim by passing a motion that stated:

THAT Lot 7 Block E, Sketch Plan 244-01, Stawamus
I.R. No. 24, reverts back to the Squamish Nation, and
Nona Lockhart be given first consideration of the Lot 7,
Block E, when allocated a home in the future.[3]

The terminology of the motion was open-ended: "in the future" avoid-
ed making any clear commitment to her. In fact, according to the Senate
Proceedings, "despite [Nona's] request [in 1989] to return to live on the
reserve, the band has not made provision for her to do so."[4] When the band
council was questioned about when she might expect to get a home on the
reserve, the council failed to answer. The band membership passed two
motions to force the council to publish the waiting list and distribute it to all
members, but by December 1999 there was still no sign of the list.

In the end the only benefit Nona Lockhart received by being reinstated was being able to confer status on her daughter, Wendy Lockhart, who
also became an official member of the band.

According to her testimony at the Senate Committee hearings in
May 1999, Wendy Lockhart "wrote to John Watson [regional director

general of Indian and Northern Affairs] with specific questions about [federal] government funds for the Squamish Nation housing program." She received a reply dated January 6, 1999, from Ernie Filzwieser, funding services officer for Indian and Northern Affairs, that:

> I am not able to respond to your questions, The Department of Indian and Northern Affairs does for the most part not keep the information at the level of detail you are requesting.[5]

Nona Lockhart died on February 8, 2009, still living off reserve. She had not obtained any resolution regarding her property claims or her request to return home.

Nona Lockhart's story was certainly not the only unhappy housing story to arise on the Squamish Nation reserves after the passage of Bill C-31. In 1986 Melva Billy, who had lived on the Stawamus reserve since 1966, was left homeless when the family home burned. The insurance company paid out $70,000 to the band, but the money was not used to replace her home. "I was told to my face it's because I'm non-native," she said, "even if all my children and grandchildren are status Squamish band members."[6] She was reduced to living in a shack she bought for one dollar. Her running water came from a garden hose and her toilet was divided from her kitchen by a thin curtain. She and her ex-husband were on good terms, but although he had undisputed title to a large chunk of the Stawamus Reserve, she could not build a home there because the Squamish band council had built five houses and a Shaker church on that land.

On October 1, 1989, Melva filed a complaint against the band council with the Canadian Human Rights Commission, which then applied to the trial division of the Federal Court of Canada. On October 7, 1994, her claim was dismissed on the grounds that "Section 67 of the Canadian Human Rights Act insulates [Indian] councils from complaints against decisions made under the Indian Act."[7] Fortunately, media coverage of the family's plight elicited widespread support, and in 1997 Melva hired a lawyer. As a result, in December 1998 Chief Bill Williams acknowledged that the band recognized the Billy family's title to the land, despite the church and houses the band had built on it. The council then offered the family five lots of reserve land if they surrendered title and gave up their right to compensation, but it would not guarantee to build a house for them.

This kind of incident was fuel to Mazie's freshly ignited political fire. She had already fought chiefs and council over her brother's home and experienced precisely the same kind of brazen behind-closed-doors property shuffling. She pointed out:

> Not many band members know that we are not covered by the Canadian Charter of Rights and Freedoms. We can't go and complain about our chiefs and council because the *Indian Act* is supposed to cover us. That Human Rights Commission is useless to us. It just means [the chiefs and councillors] can do what they want. Guess we're not Canadians — and then they want us to have self-government! That would just give council even more power over us. They would just be able to do whatever they want … Well, they do now, but then it would be legal! The old chiefs would never have treated the people this way.

Although Bill C-31 had reinstated many women to their full Indian status, it quickly became obvious that the act still discriminated against them. The young woman who finally got the federal government's attention on this issue was Sharon McIvor, a law student, whose parents were members of the Lower Nicola Band outside the town of Merritt, BC. When McIvor married a non-Native in 1970, she lost her Indian status and the son she subsequently gave birth to could not be registered as Indian. When Bill C-31 changed the rules, she applied for status for herself and for her son, but she was informed that she could only be reinstated under section 6(2), because both her parents had been products of a union between a Native and a non-Native. McIvor's son was not eligible for Indian status. However, both of McIvor's parents had actually been born out of wedlock and neither of their fathers had been acknowledged as non-Indian, and under Bill C-31 the illegitimate children of Indian women were considered status Indians. Thus, McIvor had strong grounds for reinstatement for herself *and* her son, but when she asked the board for a review of the decision, she was left waiting for twenty-one months before being advised that the original decision would stand.

McIvor then launched a court challenge on the grounds of gender discrimination. She based her case on the fact that under Bill C-31 a man who married a non-Indian kept his status and his wife was given Indian status. Their child— whether born before or after Bill C-31 was passed— also qualified for status. If this child married a non-Indian and had a child (grandchild to the first man), that child would also be granted status. Therefore, in the case of a male, Bill C-31 allowed status to three generations. Under the same bill, an Indian woman who had married a non-Indian could now have her status reinstated, and her child would also be entitled to status, but if that child married a non-Indian, his/her children could not have status. This meant that in the case of a woman only two generations would have status. McIvor also challenged the constitutionality of the *Indian Act* relating to registration as she said it discriminated against women on the basis of sex contrary to the Charter of Rights and Freedoms. It took seventeen years for the McIvor case to come to trial in the BC Supreme Court, but that court finally confirmed that both Sharon and her son had the right to full Indian status under section 6(1). At the same time the court held that section 6 of the *Indian Act* violated the Charter of Rights and Freedoms as well as international conventions on human rights, women's rights and children's rights. In June 2007, Judge Carol Ross wrote that:

> In drawing a distinction between male and female ancestors in determining who can be registered as a status Indian, section (6) offends the basic notion of human dignity. The section implies that one's female ancestors are deficient, or less Indian, than their male contemporaries. The implication is that one's lineage is inferior. The implication for an Indian woman is that she is inferior, less worthy of recognition. It seems to me that it is one of our most basic expectations that we will acquire the cultural identity of our parents, and that as parents, we will transmit our cultural identity to our children.

The federal government appealed the decision, and although the BC Court of Appeal upheld the basic findings of discrimination, they said the trial court had gone too far in dictating the solutions and gave Parliament twelve months to implement new legislation that would remove the discrimination in the act. On December 15, 2010, Bill C-3, *Gender Equity in Indian Registration Act*, received royal assent and came into force six weeks later. It ensures that eligible grandchildren of women who lost status as a result of marrying non-Indian men will become entitled to registration (Indian status) in accordance with the *Indian Act*.

However, while Bill C-31 and the McIvor case were resolving status questions, they were also affecting band membership codes. The Squamish Nation had created its first membership code in 1987, but almost immediately concerns had been raised regarding the interpretation of the phrase "natural born" as used in the code, and changes had been made accordingly. However, concerns remained regarding newly reinstated women only being allowed to return to the reserve if they were divorced or widowed, and in 1992 the band began a process of community consultation to make suggestions for improvement. Five years later a referendum was held that provided the band with a mandate to make the changes the community had recommended. These changes were approved in July 2000, and the new "2000 Membership Code" was adopted. More consultations began after Bill C-3 was passed because the code still contained unintentional discrimination in the descent and lineage rulings. It is still not complete.

The issue of Native women's rights has been tightly interwoven with the development and implementation of all the changes to the Indian Act and to band membership codes. Throughout the process it became apparent that Native women were no longer willing to sit on the sidelines as spectators. They now demanded to be treated with respect, to be heard and to participate in decisions affecting their own and their families' lives.

14

"Where's our money?'" was the headline on the front page of the *Province* newspaper on November 16, 1999. Below that headline the face of Mazie Baker stares out, and the look on that face — a look so familiar to Squamish band councillors and anyone else she had crossed swords with — says, "Don't mess with me!"

Mazie's latest battle with the council had begun in the summer of 1998 when community members began asking about the management of the band's annual budget of $32 million and decisions that were being made concerning the band's land resources. Why, members asked, were they being kept in the dark about how their money was being spent? Why wouldn't their chiefs and councillors explain where their money was going?

When that information was not forthcoming, at a general meeting held on September 21, 1998, Wendy Lockhart put forward a motion — supported by Mazie — that there should be a forensic audit of the band's financial activities. The motion was passed with 92 in favour, 43 opposed. However, the Squamish band had long ago instituted a rule that any motion to be decided by the membership had to be voted on twice. Bill Williams, who was a chief at that time, explained that this was because the Nation had many complex issues and a large membership, and thus two votes were required to come to a resolution on important issues. The second vote was held on September 29, and the results were very different: 36 members in favour, 147 opposed and 29 abstained. What happened? Why did so many more people attend the second meeting? Why were so many of them opposed? Chief Joe Mathias told the *North Shore*

News that the band's council could not agree to a forensic audit because it would cost $300,000 to $400,000, which would be a waste of money as it would only confirm what their auditors had already said.

Mazie was not going to sit quietly and accept these excuses, and she and other concerned members of the community organized a petition asking for an investigation into inadequate financial reporting to members, conflict of interest and rampant favouritism. Over a hundred band members, under the collective name of the Concerned Members of the Squamish Nation, signed this petition and sent it to Ottawa. On October 14, 1999, the group received a reply to their request for a forensic audit from L. Denis Desautels, FCA, who represented the office of the Auditor General of Canada. It was couched in the careful, non-committal official language of government and assured them that their allegations regarding the management of the Squamish Nation were important. A copy of a report to the House of Commons, dated 1999, that was included with the letter stated that the Department of Indian Affairs and Northern Development (DIAND) would give due consideration to any observations and allegations reported by First Nations. But Desautels then explained that, although the Auditor General's office did audit the DIAND, they did not have a mandate to carry out forensic audits on First Nations. He believed the department had a responsibility, he said, for the adequate resolution of allegations raised by concerned community members, especially as they related to funds supplied by Parliament, but they could not intervene in specific cases. However, he would take their concerns to the ongoing audits of the department.

These vague indications of interest expressed in "governmentese" plus the news that DIAND could not or would not intervene clearly told Mazie and her group that they were on their own. But Mazie was furious. "They treat us like dummies," she said.

The next step for the group was to go public, and this generated extensive media coverage, including the photo and two-page spread in the *Province* newspaper as well as a major headline, a front-page story and a two-page inside spread in the *North Shore News*. This publicity in turn involved the chiefs and councillors as well as the DIAND because a *North Shore News* reporter had contacted a DIAND representative to ask what action the government was going to take on these major complaints from the Squamish Nation members. The reply was that the petition was still being reviewed by ministry officials and, when they finished their review, the minister would decide if the petition should be passed on to the RCMP, who would then decide if a forensic audit was warranted.

The band council quickly responded by sending out a newsletter entitled "Communication for the Nation" to the band's members in which they said the "claims of fraud, corruption and financial mismanagement on the part of your Council and Administration … are based on unproven allegations by several members of the Squamish Nation." The letter also included an overview of the band's financial activities for the year ending March 31, 1999. Chief Bill Williams then advised the *North Shore News* that audited statements were available in the band office for any member to see. Mazie reacted with anger:

> Who would go there and ask to see audit statements? Not me. I can't even read them, and even if I could, I wouldn't be able to understand them. Council knows that. It's a safe offer to make to the people. They know nobody will go. They'd be way too scared and embarrassed.

It was the contention of Mazie and her team that copies of the financial statements should be sent out to members so that they could read them in the privacy of their homes. The band members were, they said, just like shareholders in a company, and company shareholders weren't expected to go into the head office to read the annual financial statement. Meanwhile, the team would continue to push for an investigation because they knew that sooner or later the general public was going to start asking why conditions on reserves were so bad and why education levels were so low and — especially — what was happening to their tax dollars.

Despite their failure to get a forensic audit at that time, Mazie and her group continued to be thorns in the side of the chiefs and councillors of the Squamish Nation, and in 2001 they caught the public's attention again when they renewed their complaints about the housing situation on the reserves and denounced the high salaries of some of the councillors and staff. Their timing was right because a wave of discontent was rising from First Nations people right across the country about the exorbitant salaries, smart homes and cars of their councillors while so many band members suffered in poverty and lived in homes that were falling apart. Once again Mazie and her team did what they had done so well in the past: they took their story to the media and the people.

On September 30, 2001, the *Province* newspaper produced a Sunday special with a two-page spread under the headline: Why do I live in squalor while others live it up?

Under it was a photo of Mark Antone in his home on the Mission reserve, a home that had been condemned by engineers. A second photo shows Mazie and her niece Wendy Lockhart standing outside a large well-kept house. Mazie fumed, "They make sure they have nice homes and good wages. How can somebody sit half a block away in a great big house and look down on Mark's house that's falling apart?" And she recalled:

> Mark grew up in that house. When his dad [Mazie's brother, Jimmy] died in July 1991, he got it. It's the same house where Gloria was living in the early '80s when Riannon was a baby. It was really cold and drafty and the baby would get sick, and then in the summer you cooked in there 'cause it was so hot. It was one of those houses built by Indian Affairs, you know, no insulation — cheap, cheap, cheap. They were staying with Mark 'cause they were waiting for their own house. I had to fight then to get a safe home for her and her baby. Mark's been waiting fourteen years to get it fixed. One minute he's high on the list because it's been condemned, and then there's no money or too many others need a house.

Chief Bill Williams was approached by the *Province* for a statement in response to band members' accusations, and the newspaper reported:

> Chief Bill Williams told the *Province*, "We're in the midst of a severe housing crisis, with a waiting list of over 800 people. People wait for decades or get old before they come up." He said that the band builds 15 homes a year at a cost of $80,000 [each], of which $19,000 is provided

by Indian Affairs. Members who have money can augment that.

Figures obtained by the *Province* show the Squamish band built only 49 homes from 1996–2000 [an average of 10 houses per year], although Indian Affairs provided more than $1.3 million for housing. In 1990 no homes were built, although Indian Affairs provided $590,070. In 1999 only one house was built, although Ottawa gave Squamish $462,321 to build housing.

Williams said that the band doesn't get enough dollars for infrastructure, such as sewer and water services, so can't build houses every year. He said the funds are held in reserve until the houses for which they were intended are built.

Mazie was not buying any of this. She was adamant that the band could afford to repair the homes of Mark and others in the same predicament. Whether the media coverage and the pressure it created were responsible is not known, but Mark Antone did eventually get a new home.

15

In May 1999 Mazie Baker went to Ottawa to be heard by the powerful Standing Senate Committee on Aboriginal Affairs. But her journey actually began one Friday evening in December 1998 when she was channel surfing. She had left the room and gone into her kitchen to make tea when she heard a voice on the Cable Public Affairs Channel (CPAC) she thought she recognized. She went back into her sitting room and saw that the voice belonged to Harold Calla, the director of finance for the Squamish Nation, who was in Ottawa discussing something called the *First Nations Land Management Act*. At that time she had no idea what this act was, but she did not like what she was hearing:

> He was sitting there saying, "Oh, Squamish wants this and Squamish wants that." You know, he said, "We're ready for self-government and we want it now." This was news to me! I phoned my niece Wendy Lockhart to find out if she had heard about this self-government stuff he was talking about. Then on Monday I went down to the band office and I was just fuming when I got down there. "What the hell is going on here? What is this self-government coming in to our Squamish Nation, and who sent that guy back there to Ottawa? He's not our speaker. You know the people have to vote somebody in there to go speak for us. Who gave him the right to speak for me and my family?" Surprise, surprise, they didn't have an answer for me.

Meanwhile, Wendy Lockhart, having caught a discussion on radio station CKNW about the same act, contacted her Member of Parliament, John Cummins, whose office staff found her a copy of Bill C-49: *The First Nations Land Management Act* as well as a copy of the *Framework Agreement on First Nations Land Management*, which underlay the act. With these documents in hand, Mazie and Wendy learned that Bill C-49 concerned self-government and the Squamish Nation was listed in the schedule of fourteen First Nations from across Canada who had signed the framework agreement to take over the management and control of their lands and resources. Representatives from the Squamish Nation and the other thirteen First Nations as well as the minister of Indian Affairs and Northern Development had signed the last page of the schedule on February 12, 1996. This was almost three years before Mazie happened to hear the discussion on CPAC, and it was clear that talks must have been going on between Indian Affairs and these First Nations representatives for a long time before that.

Mazie was steaming mad. The Squamish Nation's band council had been working behind the members' backs to give them self-government! Her father-in-law, Willie Baker, who had encouraged her to go to council meetings when she was young, had warned her many years ago about revisions to the *Indian Act* that would assimilate the Indians into western culture. She remembered him saying:

> "You guys are gonna get wiped out of your reserve," he said. "You won't be Indians anymore." I never really knew what he meant or which act he was talking about — I think he called it the '73 Act. And this Bill C-49 looked like what he warned me about all those years ago.

In fact, Willie Baker had probably been referring to the enfranchisement section of the *Gradual Civilization Act* of 1857, which became section 86 of the 1876 *Indian Act*, a key part of the federal government's long-term scheme to eliminate Native culture, assimilate Aboriginals into Canadian society and ultimately rid the country of the "Indian problem." *It* provided that, in exchange for accepting the privilege of voting and gaining full Canadian citizenship, an Indian person would receive "a suitable allotment" of reserve land, which he would then hold in fee simple like any other Canadian landholder. The government would thereby gain one self-sustaining, tax-paying citizen while at the same time whittling down the size of the reserve he came from. The act also made enfranchisement compulsory for any Indian who became a doctor, lawyer or notary public or who took holy orders or served in the armed forces. To the government's surprise this offer had not been received with a great deal of enthusiasm. There was no stampede of people from the reserves to become "Canadian" — in fact, only one Native person in the whole country took up the offer.

Mazie was not averse to being Canadian:

> I always tell my kids that I think why we're in this mess and treated without respect is because I don't think we are thought of as Canadian. I've never heard them call us Canadian like they do with the Native Americans. I've never heard anybody say, "Oh, you know, the Canadian Indians ..." The only thing they got right in the national anthem is "our home and *native* land." We could be called the First People, that would be okay, but this Bill C-49 has got me scared.

Unlike the original *Indian Act*, Bill C-49: *The First Nations Land Management Act* was aimed, not at individuals, but at native bands as a whole. As Mazie and her niece worked their way through the documents, they got a fairly good grasp of the overall objectives, but the key points that jumped out at them were contained in the framework agreement:

> The *Framework Agreement* provides these 14 First Nations with the option to manage their reserve lands outside the *Indian Act*. The option to regain control of their land can only be taken with the consent of the community. Only when each of these First Nations takes control of its lands and resources under the Agreement, shall federal administration of its reserve lands cease under the *Indian Act*.
>
> A First Nation signatory to the *Framework Agreement* exercises its land management option by creating

its own Land Code, drafting a community ratification
process and entering into a further Individual Transfer
Agreement with Canada. The specific steps are set out in
the *Framework Agreement.*

Despite the legal language, when the documents were read aloud to
her, Mazie immediately grabbed onto the statement that: "The option
to regain control of their land can only be taken with the consent of the
community." She knew that her community had not given its consent
because there had been no meetings to inform the people about it, and
no vote had been taken permitting the band council to begin negotiating
with the government. She also understood that the council was required
to develop something called a "land code" for the Squamish Nation, and
she didn't trust this council to do that for the good of the whole community. With their previous track record when it came to property rights, she
realized she could lose her land to them. Even though the community
would have to approve the land code by voting on it before the council
could go ahead with it, nobody in the community — except for some of
the council members — was aware that this act was even in the works.
And by now it was being debated in the House of Commons. Although
the Concerned Members of the Squamish Nation group was still deeply
involved in the problems of governance and accountability, they immediately started working on informing the people about the *Land Management
Act* and what was happening there.

Their offensive began with an opinion editorial by Wendy Lockhart
that was published in February 1999 in the *National Post* under the heading:
"Native managed lands: a threat to women." This caught the attention of
Dianne Rinehart, a reporter for the *Vancouver Sun,* who had earlier written a long article about governance and accountability on the reserves. On
February 27, 1999, the *Sun* published Rinehart's article on Bill C-49 and
headlined it with: "Reserve land bill opposed by natives and non-natives."
The sub-heading read: "Critic Mike Scott, mayors, aboriginal women op-
pose Native land bill." Interviews with Rafe Mair on radio station CKNW
and on the Aboriginal Peoples Television Network (APTN) also served
to spread the word within the Squamish Nation. An article by Suzanne
Fournier, a staff reporter for the *Province* newspaper was published on April

25, 1999, under the headline, "Natives fear for their land. Bill C-49 gives band councils too much power, women say." *The Globe and Mail, National Post, Vancouver Sun* and *Province* all printed photos, letters, and comments from Mazie and Wendy Lockhart. This extensive media coverage generated heated discussion with Natives and non-Natives alike, allowing their concerns to be heard by the general public. The exposure also drew other influential women into the fray. One of them was Barbara Wyss, a Squamish Nation elder with a background in teaching and community planning; she lives on the Capilano Reserve and is a member of Vancouver Campus of the Nicola Valley Institute of Technology's Elder Council.

The band council, still bruised by the media coverage over the call for a forensic audit just the year before, eventually spoke out through its spokesman, Chief Bill Williams, who insisted that the people of the Squamish Nation were ready for the responsibility of writing their own land laws. But Mazie and her team had a head of steam up now. They were going to find out what was really going on and make sure the people knew what was happening behind their backs. They made up letters and sent them out to the people asking if they knew anything about this Bill C-49 and what was being decided in their name. The answer came back that they didn't. The next step was a typical Mazie strategy: organize the people to attend a band council meeting.

> We all went up to a meeting with the councillors, and I stood up and asked, "How many of you councillors know about this self-government? Do you know if we're going into it?" I asked each one of them, and they said they didn't really know what it was all about. But they had to know something, or some of them did.
>
> Then me and Wendy went up to see the mayor of North Van. And he said, "Well, you know if you go into self-government, there is no way you are going to be able to use any of our facilities like the hospital and the sports fields. If you have self-government, you build your own." And I said, "Where are we going to get the money to do that?" And he said, "Well, that's what self-government means."

The two women then decided to organize a petition to send to Ottawa stating that the Squamish people knew nothing of the *Framework Agreement on the First Nations Land Management Act* or Bill C-49 that had been signed on their behalf. Mazie said:

> We went down to the smoke shop and stopped people and asked them to sign the petition. We had over 250 signatures within an hour. Now, what does that tell you? At first people didn't realize what it all meant. I told them, "We go into self-government right now, it's a big mistake. If the council can't handle the millions we get from the federal government now, imagine what will happen when they get one lump sum! It's only a one-time payment, and once you're in, you can't go back and say, 'Sorry. I don't like this.' Where are we gonna get the money to build a school, a hospital, even a jail? What about hydro and water? What happens when they've spent all the money? I haven't even heard of any plans yet for us to make our own money and create some jobs. Well, we have those leases with Park Royal and some others, but you can't run the nation, feed, clothe, and take care of the people on that! Nope, I just don't think this council can handle self-government," I said. "We'd be broke in no time," I told them.

Armed with their petition, Mazie and Wendy headed for the office of Mazie's Member of Parliament, Ted White of the Reform Party. They explained to him that they had been totally unaware of the legislation, hadn't voted on it and wanted it withdrawn — or at least have the Squamish Nation taken off the list. White tabled their petition in the House of Commons where he not only read it into the record but also commented on the contents. Mike Scott, the member for Skeena, who was the Reform Party's critic for Indian Affairs and Northern Development, also spoke in the House on their behalf.

Then in the spring of 1999 Senator Pat Carney had her staff contact them to ask for more information and confirm the facts on the issues they had raised. This proved to be the beginning of a long and helpful relationship. Her staff helped with research, distributed their correspondence, kept the team updated on events in Ottawa and kept their issues before the Senate. She also forwarded their names to policy groups for hearings and events that she thought they should attend or speak at. And when she learned that they had been unsuccessful in obtaining travel funding to speak at events or contact other Canadian Aboriginal women who were facing the same difficulties, she suggested that they should organize into a more formal group that could more easily access funding. As a result of her advice, *Native Women CARE* (Communication Accountability Respect Equality) came into being. It was also Senator Carney who made sure Mazie and Wendy were called as witnesses at the Senate hearings, while Ted White was instrumental in dealing with the administrative requirements for attending those hearings.

And then miraculously everything was finally in place. They were to appear in front of the Senate Standing Committee on Aboriginal Peoples on May 4, 1999. The official title for the day's hearings was: "Issue 28: the Fifth and Sixth meetings on Bill C-49, *the First Nation Land Management Act* and the 24th meeting on Aboriginal self-government." Senator Pat Carney had laid on everything they needed, including the use of her office phone, much to Mazie's delight.

Wendy had prepared an in-depth package for the committee to review, including letters and other documents relevant to the issues they would be discussing. The two women had then spent hours preparing a seamless presentation that would clearly delineate their many concerns regarding Bill C-49. Their presentation would follow that of the Squamish Nation band council, represented by Chief Joe Mathias, Chief Bill Williams and Harold Calla plus their legal counsel, Bill Henderson, who would be attending as members of the Interim Lands Advisory Board, and these men would remain in the room while they spoke. There would also be many other chiefs and organizations from across Canada there as witnesses. However, Mazie was not in the least concerned by this; she was going to Ottawa on a mission and no one was going to intimidate her!

It had been a long, steep flight for Mazie Baker, a woman who could neither read nor write, a member of the "lost generation" of Native peoples, from her early days of fighting for a street light on North Vancouver's

Third Street to the rarefied atmosphere of a Senate committee room in Ottawa. Although she had always been a fighter, this was a new kind of fighting, a kind where every word was going to count. But Mazie had never been intimidated by any official, whether local, provincial or federal, and she was ready to speak her mind to these senators:

> Me and Wendy had to sit at the end of a long table and all the senators and the chair sat around it, and they said, "Well, we need to ask you some questions." And I said, "Well, I'm willing as long as I understand what you are saying. I'll do my best."

The chairman of the committee that the women faced was Senator Charlie Watt from Kuujjuaq (Fort Chimo) in northern Quebec. In the 1970s he had served as an officer for the Department of Indian and Northern Affairs, but over the next decade he had been busy founding Air Inuit, Canada's first Aboriginal-owned airline, while at the same time serving as chairman of three other Native-owned companies. Watt was the first president of the Northern Quebec Inuit Association and its successor, Makivik Corporation, and he was instrumental in making sure that Aboriginal rights were recognized in the *Canadian Constitution Act* of 1982. He had been appointed to the Senate by Pierre Trudeau in 1984.

It was 5:15 in the evening of Tuesday, May 4, before Mazie and Wendy were invited to the table, and Wendy led off with a summary of her mother's case history to demonstrate the legitimacy of her membership in the band while at the same time deftly illustrating the Squamish band council's underhanded dealing with cases of inherited matrimonial property. This was an important point since, under C-49, First Nations councils would have complete freedom in dealing with such properties. She then turned to the legality of the council's signatures on the framework agreement for Bill C-49, pointing out that:

> Clause 45 [of Bill C-49] states that the Governor-in-Council may, by order, add the name of a band to the schedule if the Governor-in-Council is satisfied that the signing of the framework agreement on behalf of the band has been duly authorized and that the framework agreement

has been so signed. In your examination of and debate on Bill C-49, I respectfully ask you to question the basis on which the Governor-in-Council was or would be satisfied that the signing of the framework agreement on behalf of the Squamish Nation had been duly authorized when, in fact, it was not even provided to members for information. I respectfully ask you to question the legal validity of the framework agreement when council was not mandated to sign it and members did not vote in a referendum, unlike some signatory bands, to indicate their participation.

I respectfully ask you to query why it is that, on the one hand, we have a treaty negotiation process in which a statement of intent confirms the mandate from the people to negotiate a treaty leading to ratification by the

Mazie in charge of Canada, ruling from Senator Pat Carney's office in Ottawa. Photo: Family collection, Keith Nahanee Jr.

membership of the framework agreement, yet on the other hand we have an agreement pursuant to Bill C-49 that was *not* ratified by the people nor even provided to them for information. I was also not advised that the Squamish Nation went to Ottawa to support Bill C-49. Having read a copy of the transcript from the Standing Senate Committee on Aboriginal Peoples held December 2, 1998, I was shocked that representations regarding the future of the Squamish Nation, which will affect my position and my rights as a member, were being made on my behalf without my knowledge. I was stunned to learn that council has a list of projects totaling $1.3 billion in activity to develop Squamish Nation lands. I have never seen this list or been provided with information about these plans.

Wendy then proceeded to skewer one of the band members who had spoken for the band earlier that day:

Harold Calla, in addressing your committee, introduced his son and stated that "Jason is obviously a member of the Squamish Nation." I am of the same generation as Harold Calla and both of our mothers are returning Bill C-31 women who had married non-Native men. My son, Maximilian Lundberg, is not a member of the Squamish Nation, and according to a letter dated February 25, 1999, from Indian Affairs, my son is not entitled to be registered under the Indian Act. These facts are relevant to your examination of Bill C-49 because they are evidence of a pattern of discrimination against Native women in terms of a significant property issue — inheritance. If I were able to inherit my grandfather's property from my mother, I could not pass the land on to my son because he is considered to be non-native and a non-member. The only way that I could have the same inheritance rights as all other Canadian women is if Bill C-31 were to be amended to provide for all descendants of native women to be made status band members. Bill C-31 fails because it only specifies that the children of returning women are eligible for status and band membership, not all of their descendants. Alternatively if the structure of land holdings for Natives were the same as for other Canadians — in other words, if the land was held in fee simple — then inheritance rights would be equal ...

On the issue of Native women's property rights on marriage breakdown, the Squamish Nation even intervened on behalf of all the signatory bands on the side of the federal government and against the BC Native Women's Society's lawsuit against Bill C-49 without informing band members. In view of this, I am absolutely convinced that Native women's property rights will not be dealt with in a fair manner and will not be equal to all other Canadian women in the band's own land code under Bill C-49 ... I am concerned that clause 28(1) would legislate power to the council to expropriate land for First Nations purposes that are not defined ...

In fact, the way that the power to expropriate was defined in the Act was wide open to interpretation; as long as the band council said the land was needed for the benefit of the Nation or for perceived planning needs, it seemed there would be no way for an individual to fight the council's decision to take their land. Wendy continued:

I am concerned that clause 12(2) regarding approval of land codes and agreements requires a minimum participation of eligible voters of only 25 percent. In terms of the Squamish Nation, this represents approximately the number of members who are employed by the band, and in my experience of trying to participate in band business in a truly democratic fashion, this is another particularly worrisome clause ... Clause 20(3) deals with search and seizure, but does not specify the federal laws with which Bill C-49 should be consistent ...

Wendy Lockhart concluded her presentation by saying:

> I am opposed to a bill that would give more power to a First Nation council that has not behaved responsibly in 14 years and returned a Native woman's property to her. I am concerned that council's powers of expropriation will displace many band members and that claims such as my mother's will just disappear. As a status member, I consider Squamish Nation participation in Bill C-49 and the framework agreement legally invalid and not binding as the criteria pursuant to clause 45 were not met because the signing of the framework agreement was not duly authorized on behalf of the band. I therefore submit that the Squamish Nation should be removed from the schedule of First Nations. I respectfully ask you to consider, honourable senators, in your examination and debate on Bill C-49, that legally binding provisions that would restore and in some cases even establish human and property rights for Native women, Native men and non-Natives on First Nations land equal to all other Canadians would be much better served through an openly debated treaty process.[8]

It was now Mazie's turn to speak, and while Wendy's job had been to deal with the legal aspects of their protest, Mazie was to present the human side of the problem:

> Honorable senators, I am very pleased to be here to speak on behalf of my people. I don't know where to begin. I found out about Bill C-49 when I saw Harold Calla talking on television about how the Squamish Nation wants this and how the Squamish Nation wants that. It just blew me away. It tore me apart to see him speaking that way. He said that the Squamish Nation will do wonders for its people. They talk about how wonderful they will be for their people, but they are never there. They are always fighting against the people.

They say, "Oh, we took people out of the welfare lineup and put them in the stupid store [Mazie's name for the Real Canadian Superstore on the Seymour Reserve] to work." They say, "We took eighty people off welfare." For how many days? They maybe work for this store one day. Then they do not care if they work at all again. That is how they are. They do not look after our people. They just keep saying, "We will look after our people," but they are never there for us. They are always fighting against us.

We have to fight for our language, culture, education and elders. I have petitions here from my people saying, "We do not want Bill C-49." Has Harold ever brought any petitions to you and said this is what our people want? I do not think he has one petition. But this is what I brought for you today. I have so many people concerned about Bill C-49.

Chairman Charlie Watt interrupted to ask, "Would you consider tabling that with the committee?" And Mazie said:

Yes. I could have had more, but when I wanted to tell my people what was happening with this Bill C-49, our chiefs and council locked us out of all our recreation centres, elder centres and learning centres. We had no place to meet. We could not even talk about it. That is how they work against the people. If you pass Bill C-49, I am telling you that it will ruin our people. They are just healing from the residential schools. If this bill goes through, you will bring them right back down to their knees because they have been through having that land taken away from them and used for money.

I have some of my CPs here, which I own. If this bill goes through, what is the use of my having them? I am trying to will them to my children, but I cannot because if that bill goes through, I might as well just rip them up right here. I am telling you that this bill is not meant for the Squamish Nation. It will never work. Our people are suffering. I told them that the rich get richer and the poor get poorer — and it is time to stop them from getting what they want. If this is the only way we can do it, let us do it. I know this bill will ruin my people and I speak for them. They always say that I am the leader and I speak for them. I have much backing from the elders, and even the younger generations have come to me, but if you ask Harold and Bill if they have anybody backing them up, they would say no because no one does. All they do is fight each other. We tried to organize a general meeting, and as soon as we called it, they cancelled it. We cannot hold a meeting. If we can prevent the passage of this bill, then I hope to make a better life for my people. I will give them back the gyms that belong to them. We cannot use them because they have the keys. They want to charge us $500 to $800 to use them. Where would we get $500 to $800 to rent a gym? We do not have that kind of money. Our kids are out on the streets today because those doors are locked against them. They cannot get in. If they want to use a gym, they have to pay $16 an hour. Where will welfare kids get that kind of money? We are just so tired of this going on and on. As I said, the rich get rich and the poor get poorer. That is the only way to see it …

They say we are the rich Squamish Nation, but I say prove it to me. We have land leases here and there, but where does the money go? Every time we go to the band office and ask for some money, we are told that we are broke. We have no money. Yet they want a raise in their wages and the money comes just like that to them — but not to us.

We tried to get an audit done on our band finances. They would not allow it. They threatened our people that they would be cut back on this and cut back on that. Our people become scared because they do not know what to do. They threaten them by saying, "If you do this, we are going to cut back on education. If you do that, we will cut back for the language program and we will cut back on welfare." They want to cut back everything but they never cut back on their own wages. They stay high. We get $32 million [annually from the federal government] to run our Squamish Nation, and yet three months or seven months into the year, we are broke. I asked them, "Where does that money go? Why cannot you help our people who are struggling so hard?" I am always up there fighting these chiefs and council.

Then, glancing over at the Squamish Nation representatives sitting in the audience, she added:

You call them chiefs, but to me they are not chiefs. I never call them chiefs because they are not *my* chiefs. A chief would be standing there *with* the people, not fighting against them. Sorry if I sound rude, but that is how I see it and that is how I feel. A leader has to be a chief whom the people can respect. That is what they have lost. All the people who are supposedly working for us have lost the respect of our own people. They treat them like dirt. I hope I will change that when I get back home.[9]

Mazie paused then said, "I guess that is about it."

Watt waited a moment before asking, "Now are we free to go into questions?" The first person to raise his hand was Senator Ray Perrault. He was more familiar with the problems of BC's Native populations than some of the others around the table because he had served in the BC legislature as leader of the Liberal Party from 1960 to 1968 and as a Liberal Member of Parliament from 1968 to 1972. He had been appointed to the Senate in 1973. Perrault complimented the two women on presenting "an excellent brief, well organized and well put together," but he was alarmed at their "allegations of serious abuse." If this abuse really was occurring, he said, the committee needed a list of changes or amendments that the women would like to see in order to take their complaints to the Justice Department. Wendy responded:

I can draw up a list for you if you like. However, over and above that, there is the fact that Bill C-49 went forward without it going to the people first.

Perrault:

You are saying there was inadequate consultation.

Wendy:

There was *no* consultation. I understand that some of the other signatory bands did actually hold referenda. If that is the case and that is what the people in those bands want, that is fine.

Perrault:

Did you have a town hall meeting?

Wendy:

We had no meetings at all. I found out about it in October when I heard something on the radio. I phoned my MP's office and got information. They sent me a copy of the bill. I was shocked to see the Squamish Nation listed there because I had not been given any information about it by my own band. I have never participated in a vote on it. As I said, I have been a very responsible and diligent band member. I have attended meetings, council meetings and cultural events, but I have never been advised by the band council or a band member of any proposed legislation, the framework agreement or Bill C-49. Nothing. And with regard to section 45 [of the bill] if ABC Corporation wanted to merge with XYZ Corporation, would the shareholders not have to approve that? In our case, there was no vote, no referendum, and no documentation. The people were not given the information. Bill C-49 was negotiated in secret. The people knew nothing about it.

Perrault:

You had no invitations to participate?

Wendy:

> I have never been advised by the band council or a band member of any proposed legislation, the framework agreement or Bill C-49. Nothing.[10]

Then one by one the senators around the table hammered away with questions, not so much disbelieving the women as trying to understand the lack of consultation on the part of the band council. Were Wendy and Mazie quite sure they had known nothing about the First Nations Land Management agreement before hearing about it via the media? After all, it had been signed three years earlier. Are band meetings advertised? Although the band may not send out individual letters to people, are there notices of meetings on public bulletin boards or in the local newspapers? If Bill C-49 was amended to make the terms of expropriation similar to expropriation of any other land in Canada, would that improve property rights? Then Mazie was asked to explain how property rights were obtained on reserves. Do you purchase it or is it given to you? After she explained the certificate of possession system, Inuit Senator Willie Adams, appointed in 1977, asked:

> You have a lot number. As soon as you acquire your land, no one can take it away from you. I do not know how the system works on the reserve, but any member of your band should tell you that you are entitled to that piece of property. How could you lose it?

Mazie:

> My brother had a lot there. He was in jail and some people just came and took his lot and started building a home on it. They did not even ask him. We are going through the court system because this is what happens to all our people's land. They know it is yours, yet they have the gall to go and build homes on it. That's how our chiefs and council behave.

Senator David Tkachuk of Saskatchewan, appointed in 1993, still concerned that the Squamish band council had not consulted with the people, commented:

> I am very surprised to hear there was no consultation. We have been told that there was consultation with the membership. To be very clear, are you saying that there was no public event for the discussion of Bill C-49 with the members of the band?

Wendy:

> In the late fall of 1998 we started to inform some of our members, and we wrote questions to the band and asked for information. We also wrote to the Department of Indian Affairs but received no response. We then learned about the upcoming debate in the House of Commons and we started the petition. Before the bill was dealt with in the House in February, there was a community information meeting called by the band, but notice was not sent to everyone. That meeting was not recorded and there was no vote taken on whether the members wanted to participate in the process. That meeting was attended by approximately 40 band members. A week later there was another community meeting. Again not all band members were notified. For example, my mother did not get a notice, and I got a phone call on the day of the meeting informing me that there was a meeting that night. That meeting was not recorded. There were 40 or 50 people there.

Manitoba Senator Janis Johnson, appointed in 1990, turned to Mazie:

> You have said that your son is on the band council, but that there have been no discussions or negotiations that, in your mind, are adequate. How has that happened? Do you not communicate with your son? Is he not able to tell you everything that is happening?

Mazie:

> Everything is supposed to stay in the council room. You do not discuss anything further when you are out of the room. Your power is only in that room.

Johnson:

> You are saying nothing leaves the council rooms so there are no further discussions?

Mazie:

> I would not want to ask my son about these things because it is not up to him. It is up to the chiefs and all the council to talk to the people, not just one of them.

Johnson:

> It would be helpful if you did communicate with them.

Mazie:

> What do you think we've been trying to do!

(What Mazie did *not* explain was that, when she first started on her political path, she knew her family was concerned for her safety, and she did not wish to implicate them in her battles.

> I make it a policy that me and Roy do not discuss what is going on in council or what I am planning to do. I may let him know that I'm going to a meeting, but not what it's about, even if he could have guessed. I do not want anyone to think I use my son's position to obtain inside information. He has to stay "clean," you know. I always joke around with him when I go to council meetings. I say, "I told you to stay home, son! I'm gonna raise hell here.")

Wendy interrupted the questions to draw the committee's attention back to the most important issue: the fact that the band council had not consulted with the people about the framework agreement. She said:

If you look at the document annexed to my presentation as "S," you will see it is a letter from Bill Williams in which he states that the framework agreement did *not* go to the people. Those are his own words.

Johnson:

In that respect then, I refer you to clause 10(2) of Bill C-49, which provides that "Every person who is 18 years of age or over and a First Nations member, whether or not resident on the reserve of the First Nation, is eligible to vote in the community approval process" for both the First Nation land code and individual agreement. Clause 12 of the bill sets out various methods for obtaining community approval and requires that a minimum of 25 percent of eligible voters must vote to approve a proposed land code and individual agreement. That is in the bill itself.

Wendy:

I still question the legal validity of the document on the basis of clause 45. It did not go to the people before they signed the framework agreement and before Bill C-49.[11]

This seemed to conclude the questions and Committee Chairman Watt thanked the two women again, but he added:

You do not give us much comfort in terms of where to go from here. We are finding there are many problems in regard to the position of women in general. All Bill C-49 does is give the band the flexibility to be able to deal with the question of land. They do not have that now. That rests in the hands of one minister today. They are trying to empower themselves. You elect these people and you can vote them out if you are not happy with them. Are you saying that you do not want Bill C-49, even though it goes a certain distance toward improving on the *Indian Act*?

Wendy:

> I am saying that for the Squamish nation, the agreement should go to the people first. The people should vote in a referendum, like other signatory bands, to determine whether they want to enter into the agreement. I feel that Bill C-49 is flawed in too many areas.

Watt:

> Are you saying that the Squamish Nation should not opt in right now?

Wendy:

> Right.

Saskatchewan senator Raynell Andreychuk, appointed in 1993:

> Then are you happier remaining under the dominance of a system of white man's rule, which we continue to hear you do not want?

Wendy:

> Under the *Indian Act*?

Andreychuk:

> Yes.

Wendy:

> Yes.

Mazie:

> We would rather stay there …

Wendy:

> … until there is a proper, publicly discussed treaty process.

Watt:

> Including the overall problem with women's rights.

Mazie and Wendy:

Yes.[12]

Mazie and Wendy's time before the committee was over; they'd had their say, answered questions and made suggestions. But Senator Watt asked to meet with them privately after the session closed, and there he asked further questions to clarify some of the issues that had come up in the committee room. Not surprisingly, Mazie took the opportunity to give him an earful. And they knew that he had listened to what they had to say about property and Native women's rights because the next day, May 5, he questioned the Squamish Nation's delegation about their lack of process around the framework agreement and their treatment of women. Joe Mathias answered the first part by saying:

> Why present a possibility to the 1,800–2,000 members of the Squamish Band when we have no assurance that this bill will become law? I am awaiting that eventuality with great anticipation because it will be the most exciting time in the history of the Squamish people. That will be a time to consider our own constitution in relation to controlling our land and our resources and how we deal with our women … My answer to you is we will embark upon detailed consultations with our membership and we have already had two meetings to introduce the information.

Bill Henderson, legal council for the Squamish Band, jumped into the dialogue to assure the committee that that yes, the matrimonial issue was a significant topic and that there was a mechanism in place to "ensure the protection of women's rights and ensure the protection of people of both genders, children included, both Native and non-Native."

But Senator Watt was not finished with Joe Mathias. He continued by saying:

> When some of my colleagues mentioned consulting with your people, you stated that consulting with them now — and if I am putting words in your mouth, please

correct me — would only give them high expectations that might not be realized. That is, there might not be a delivery at the end of the day because there is uncertainty as to whether this bill will be passed. If I understood you correctly, you also said that after this you will go back to your community and consult with your people, whether or not you will opt in. That is what I heard. Taking that into account, we have repeatedly heard from Native women — not only on Bill C-49 but also on the studies that we are undertaking in regard to governance — that they are being mistreated by their own people. When you consult with your own people, the opportunity will be widened in terms of attacking the other aspects that are troubling the First Nations, including women.

Mathias answered that, after the issue of the *Framework Agreement* emerged in the media, the chiefs and councillors did hold general meetings, and one person at the Squamish Valley meeting had told them he did not want to hear anything until it was law. This, he said, represented the other view, the one they had actually been following. He addressed the women's issue by suggesting that the Senate Committee he was addressing should recommend to the senators, the minister of Indian Affairs and the government of Canada that a standing committee be created to deal with the matter of First Nations' women's rights.

Senator Watt was not deflected. He continued to make his point that communication with the people was absolutely essential. Being aboriginal himself, he felt it was his responsibility to share his experiences with his people. There had been a situation within his own band where the people were passing incorrect information among themselves due to a lack of understanding, and as a result, they were not able to get together and deal with the crux of the issues that were dividing them. He said:

I should like to point out that this type of situation is not very helpful. I do not know how other senators view it, but as an aboriginal senator, it is not something that I enjoy hearing on a continuous basis. As a person who was raised by a woman who was both mother and father to me, it hurts to hear how our women — our mothers and sisters — are being treated.

He continued by telling the assembled witnesses that everyone needed to be on board if the people were to move ahead into self-government. It was crucial that the chiefs and councillors work at the local level to ensure everyone understood what was happening and what needed to be done. And he closed the two days of hearings by stating:

> There must be a closed dialogue if we are to succeed. To become a government down the road, we must work together and we must stick together. We must come with one voice and we must pray from one hymn book.[13]

The chiefs had been given due notice to go home, talk to their people and treat their women fairly and with respect. Mazie and Wendy had been heard.

In his book, *The Unjust Society*, Harold Cardinal wrote:

> We do not want the *Indian Act* retained because it is a good piece of legislation. It isn't. It is discriminatory from start to finish. But it is a lever in our hands and an embarrassment to the government, as it should be. No just society and no society with even pretensions to being just can long tolerate such a piece of legislation, but we would rather continue to live in bondage under the inequitable Indian Act than surrender our sacred rights. Any time the government wants to honour its obligations to us we are more than ready to help devise new Indian legislation.

If Mazie had been able to read this, she would have discovered she and Cardinal were in total agreement about continuing to live under the *Indian Act* until the federal government honoured its obligations to the Native population of this country. She would probably have thumped her dining room table with delight.

Mazie exultant on the steps of Parliament. "I made it all the way to Ottawa."
Photo: Family Collection, Keith Nahanee Jr.

16

Mazie and Wendy returned home from Ottawa feeling as though they had really accomplished something and that it was important to let the people know what they had learned and heard. However, some members of the council were angry that they'd had the nerve to speak out against the council in front of other chiefs, groups from across Canada and members of the Senate, and they refused to allow them to use any of the on-reserve meeting rooms. They had to hold their meeting off reserve. Mazie recalled:

> I was told I would be taken to court and sued! Can you be-
> lieve that? I said, "Go right ahead! I have nothing but rocks
> in the back of my yard and you are welcome to those!"
> What the heck were they so scared of? Losing face?

Unfortunately, in spite of Mazie and Wendy's determined drive to demonstrate to the Senate Standing Committee on Aboriginal Peoples that the Squamish people had not been consulted about the *Framework Agreement on First Nation Land Management* nor had they given the band council permission to sign it, the band's delegates were able to convince the committee that their two very recent and poorly attended "informa-tion meetings" constituted adequate consultation. As a result, the com-mittee did not recommend striking the Squamish Nation from the list of fourteen bands that had signed the agreement. The Senate submitted a few minor amendments to the House of Commons on May 13, 1999, just nine days after Mazie and Wendy had made their presentation. Bill C-49 passed third and final reading in the House the same day and was given royal assent a month later. The band council of the Squamish Nation now began work on designing the land code that would be used to manage the band's lands under self-government.

Meanwhile, neither the passage of Bill C-49 nor the threats they received caused Mazie and her team to stop their advocacy work. They continued to concentrate on legislation, governance and accountability by focussing on the negative aspects of the bill, but especially the matrimonial property issue. They were helped by a growing interest in the question by Canada's media and questions from many segments of the population, not just First Nations people. And finally, more and more women, individually and in groups right across the country, began talking about the problems with Bill C-49 in regard to Native women's property rights.

Mazie and Wendy accepted all invitations to speak to committees, groups and media. In 2000 Mazie gave a presentation about their concerns regarding Aboriginal women's rights to the Official Opposition Hearings on the Nisga'a Treaty in Vancouver. In September 2001 the two of them spoke to the Select Standing Committee on Aboriginal Affairs in the BC Legislature when that committee examined the topic of *Revitalizing the Provincial Approach to Treaty Negotiations: Recommendations for a Referendum on Negotiating Principles.* In April 2002 Wendy contributed to an article in *Homemakers Magazine* entitled "Chief Injustice: Native women stand tall to fight corruption on reserves." Both women travelled to Ottawa to participate in the meetings held in March 2002 and again in July of that year. They met Native women from across Canada who shared their experiences in their communities and their worries about their lack of legal protection for their homes. Afterwards Mazie said:

> I never thought I would be out there talking to all these people — lawyers, senators, and Native women's groups. Going to government meetings? Me? My mom would be proud, I think. I remember being scared to open my mouth in band council meetings. I guess I got over that all right. Without Wendy I wouldn't have been able to do the work the two of us do. She always made sure I understood all these bills and discussion papers. I had no idea when I said years ago I was going into politics

that my life would change so much, what it would mean for me. It really made me look real hard at what needed to be done for the people, but it was clear that someone better try to do something, and I knew deep inside it had to be me. My kids worried about me so much. They were afraid I might get hurt or something. Me? I'm not afraid of anyone, never have been. Me and Wendy, we keep on going; keep on trying.

Both women attended hearings of the Standing Committee on Aboriginal Affairs, Northern Development and Natural Resources that were held in Nanaimo in February 2003. This time the topic was yet another amendment to the *Indian Act*: Bill C-7, the proposed *First Nations Governance Act*, and they were there to voice their concerns about band governance, lack of transparency, band finances, housing conditions, and discrimination when it came to matrimonial real property. Mazie addressed all of these high-level groups undaunted by her inability to read and write. She spoke from the heart and was always impressive and memorable. She said:

> Well now, I couldn't use notes or prepare a written speech, could I? I have a really good memory, though, and I remember the facts and figures and stuff that Wendy explained to me. I just looked them the eye and told them what needs fixing.

Meanwhile, in response to the continuing pressure from media and vocal groups, the Department of Indian Affairs and Northern Development had established a Women's Gender and Equality Directorate, which then formed three focus groups to study "Matrimonial Real Property on Reserves." The long-awaited feedback from these focus groups was compiled by Wendy Corbet and Allison Lendor and published on November 28, 2002, as *The Discussion Paper: Matrimonial Real Property on Reserves*. Four years later, on October 21, 2006, the Directorate took those findings to a meeting in Saskatoon of the Indigenous Bar Association (IBA) with Indian and Northern Affairs Canada, and out of that meeting came yet another paper called *Final Conference Report Addendum on Matrimonial Real Property on Reserves*. This provided another opportunity for discussion at a high level regarding the situation of Native women on reserves.

Shortly after the release of the discussion paper, Senator Shirley Maheu put forward a motion, seconded by Senator Lise Bacon, that the Senate should look into "the situation regarding on-reserve matrimonial real property on the breakdown of marriage or common law relationship and the policy context in which they are situated." Senator Pat Carney immediately lobbied for the Senate Committee on Aboriginal Affairs to deal with the issue, but she was overruled and it became the responsibility of the Senate Human Rights Committee. The report that committee produced in November 2003 was called *A Hard Bed to Lie In: Matrimonial Property on Reserve*. It opens with the following statement:

> I believe that one of the basic rights we should be able to enjoy is the right to call a place, a community or a structure "home." Home is a place where we are safe and protected by family and friends. It is our private spot where we can lock out the cares of the world and enjoy one another. It is also the place where, as a couple, when we plan a family, we know that this is the place where they will be safe, protected and loved. As a couple, you take a structure, and with personal touches from each of you, you make this your private world. You open your private world to family and friends, making them feel welcome when they visit you.
>
> However, make no mistake: this place is your private world. Imagine the stress on a woman who knows that, if this loving relationship ends, then her world will crumble. Imagine the stress when this woman has children, and she knows that not only she but also her children will soon have to leave the place she and they call home, and in some cases, must leave the community. It is not an easy choice to decide that a relationship is not working and that the relationship must end. Normally, while there is a certain degree of animosity, most couples know that they must work out a mutually agreed upon arrangement for the disposition of property, including the home.

> This would not appear to be the case for on-reserve women, as they hold no interest in the family home. There is no choice as to who has to move. It is the woman and, in most cases, it is the woman and her children. What a choice: be homeless or be in a loveless relationship, maybe an abusive relationship. Is that what Aboriginal women deserve? No, it is not. Is it humane? It is definitely not.[14]

The report was read to Mazie from cover to cover, and her reaction was:

> Well, someone in government seems to be listening. It's only taken them *years*. How does anything ever get done over there [Ottawa]? It's as bad as trying to get a house here … You could die before anything really happens! Now, if we women ran the country, we'd have it sorted out in no time *and* it would be fair.

Mazie grinned as she said this and her eyes twinkled, but she meant it.

All of these studies provided a foundation for the introduction of Bill S-4, the *Family Homes on Reserves and Matrimonial Rights or Interests Act*. Unfortunately, this act died on the order paper when Stephen Harper dissolved Parliament on March 26, 2011, and called a federal election for May 2.

Back home on the Mission Reserve, far from the rarefied atmosphere of government and Senate committees, Mazie somehow always found time to work on the day-to-day problems faced by her people: property disputes, governance, education, finances, accountability and language. One of the disputes she became involved in at this time concerned the band council's distribution of funds to the people. These are not monies from government funding but payments of "shares" that reflect a percentage of the band's profits from land leases and other council initiatives. At one time the distribution amount had been just $400 per year, but that was later raised to $1,000 per person, paid out in installments four times a year. As time passed, however, the cost of living rose, but the disbursement amount stayed the same, even though the band's profits had markedly increased. Mazie wanted to know why:

> A thousand dollars didn't buy the same amount of food
> and clothing for the families anymore. All those millions
> they got coming in and we get $250 four times a year! It's
> peanuts. Where does all that money go?

Mazie, Jo-Ann Nahanee and others began to petition the band council for an increase, but they failed to make any headway. Instead, the council pointed out that people on social assistance would lose their allowance if they were given an increase, and that would not be fair. Since it was exactly this group that needed the additional funds, Mazie's group then began to look at how they could be paid an increased amount without losing their social assistance allowance. They started their investigation with a meeting with Indian Affairs but learned that the department had no authority over social assistance payments. They were told it was the responsibility of the band council. They were back to square one.

Mazie's most effective tactic had always been to "take it to the people" when she was disgruntled with the band council or saw something happening to "her people" that she felt was unfair. Now she was so frustrated with the whole "distribution thing" that she went out on the reserve and talked to everyone she met, and soon people began dropping by the house to ask her for more information. She "rattled everyone's cages" to get them out to a meeting and get organized. She succeeded.

On June 13, 2010, a meeting of the people was held to discuss asking council for an increase. They were given information on the Nation's income for 2009 based on own-source revenue projection, that is, revenue not including federal transfers. Leases such as Park Royal were estimated to bring in $23 million annually, taxation $7.1 million and the marina $3 million. The projected number of members in the Nation was 4,400 at this date. Based on this information, a motion was made by Yvette John and seconded by Clarissa Antone to increase the distribution amount to $3,000 per year. The motion was passed with 144 in favour, 4 abstentions and 1 opposed.

Then in accordance with the Squamish Nation's requirement for two meetings and two votes on motions to be brought to council, Mazie organized a second meeting for September 19. Remembering previous second votes that had reversed the decision of the first vote, she and Jo-Ann covered all the bases, printing flyers that were sent out to every home and even providing a bus to take people to the meeting. But this was a subject affecting every member of the Nation, and attendance was high. The second vote was taken and again the motion was passed. Now they could go before council with the results.

Despite the overwhelming vote in favour of the increase, the band council refused to comply on the grounds that it would cost too much and be detrimental to the people on social assistance because they would lose that income. Mazie, Jo-Ann and their committee were defeated. This did not happen very often when Mazie went into battle except, it seemed, when the financial policies of the council were being questioned and changes asked for — as in the earlier call for a forensic audit. There was nowhere else to go with this one, and nothing more they could do. The voice of the people had been heard and once more disregarded.

17

Meanwhile, throughout their continued work at the local political level and their travels to address meetings on Native women's rights, Mazie and Wendy had been keeping an eagle eye on what was happening with *Bill C-49, the First Nations Land Management Act.* Although the act had received royal assent in June 1999, ten years had passed and nothing appeared to change in the Squamish Nation — as far as the women could see. They knew that activation of the *Framework Agreement* was dependent upon a land code being drawn up by the band council with community input, but in the intervening years, despite the assurances the Squamish delegates had given the Senate Committee members, there had been very little that could be called consultation with band members. They also knew that rejection of the land code by the band membership would prevent control of the land and its resources being passed to the band council, and the management of the Squamish Nation and its lands would remain under the jurisdiction of the *Indian Act.* This meant that there was still a way to defeat the band councillors and their drive for self-government. The battle was far from over.

The powerful team of Mazie Baker and Wendy Lockhart had acquired a new member by this time: Jo-Ann Nahanee, who had worked with Mazie in her dispute over her brother's house as well as on the issue of the shares disbursements. Jo-Ann had recently received a copy of a 152-page book on Bill C-49 written by BC lawyer Janice G.A.E. Switlo in June 1999. The title, *Apple Cede: First Nations Land Management Regime,* is a brilliant play on words, "apple" being a derogatory term for a non-traditional Indian (red on the outside and white on the inside) and "cede" being a term most often used when describing the surrender via treaty of a fortress or a country to an enemy. The title page of this book, which is carefully annotated and end-noted, contains the following words: *Canada's solution to decisively exterminate aboriginal title*. In her paper Switlo explains that the wording of the *First Nations Land Management Act*, Bill C-49 is open to wide interpretation, such that the passage of a land code would effectively surrender the Nation's reserve lands to the Queen since the royal proclamation of 1763 states that surrender of lands can only be made to the Queen. It would also mean that when the Nation abandons its Aboriginal title to its lands, it would be left with only residual management rights, and these residual rights would not be constitutionally protected as the Nation would no longer have Aboriginal or treaty rights.

Passing the land code and activating the *Framework Agreement* would, therefore, be a major blow to the Nation's cultural and religious beliefs. The belief that the rights to their land came from the Creator would be denied; passing the land code would be a statement that, even if they did once believe, they no longer do. It would mean that the Queen would own all the land, all the resources and all the animals. No longer would the hunters have the Creator to thank for the gift of a successful hunt. Switlo pointed out that they would have to thank the Queen:

> To those Aboriginal people who do believe, this is the ultimate betrayal, the betrayal of the Creator, who entrusted them with the care of land. Signing would deny the underlying religious creation belief of the Nation. Religious beliefs are the most highly protected international human right, protected by the Charter of Rights and Freedoms. This is why it is so important not to be signed in to the Framework Agreement, and why, if the people do not agree with this and what their chief and council have done, they must assert their continued belief through legal or other action.[15]

Jo-Ann did not like what she read, especially the renunciation of religious beliefs, and she had no recollection of the band council ever discussing this or explaining it to the people. She asked herself if the councillors were even aware of this fact or any of the other dangers hidden in the legal language of the act and the *Framework Agreement*. She decided she needed to get involved and do something to stop the passage of the land code. She said:

> I became the researcher, the reader, writer of letters to the media, to MLAs and lawyers, even one to the Queen. [Mazie's comment was: "Why not? She doesn't put on her pants any different than us!"] I was seeking information and direction, explaining the situation and asking them for support. I always read the letters to Mazie and made any changes she wanted before they were mailed.
>
> She would explain to me her point of view about what passing the land code would mean for us and our children. She would tell me, "Sometime in the future people will be driving by what used to be the Mission Reserve and they will say, 'Remember when Indians used to live here?' We will have to go out to UBC to see who we were or used to be." Mazie didn't like that future. Her focus and strength was getting the word out to "the people." She had a way of reaching out and getting them to listen and hear what she had to say.
>
> In times of disagreement her call was always, "Bring it to the people for a vote." This strategy had served her well over the years, and as a result she had earned the people's respect and trust. She tried to get them to understand they had the power, the right to vote for themselves and not vote as directed by chiefs and council. She constantly reminded them that council was supposed to represent them, the people. Her open door welcomed anyone — she was as comfortable with the bum on the street as she was with highly placed individuals. She would say what her truth was in a loving way or in a direct way or to the point, but not always what people wanted to hear, especially chiefs and council.

When the band council announced that there was to be a vote on the land code on April 7 and 8, 2011, Mazie and her team knew they had to get out and hold their information meetings as soon as possible. They approached the Pivot Legal Society for assistance, and this proved to be an excellent move as Pivot is self-described as "a legal advocacy group that fights legislation, policies and practices that undermine human rights, intensify poverty and deprive people of the opportunity to become a full and equal participant in their communities." They also contacted the Atira Women's Resource Society, a not-for-profit committed to ending violence against women, and they provided legal advice and assistance. A legal advocate from Atira also helped them draft a notice to send out to all members. It outlined their concerns about the impact of the land code on the people and asked them to vote No. It said:

> VOTE NO on APRIL 7–8, 2011
>
> RE: THE SQUAMISH LAND CODE.
>
> Recently we have all received a package from the chief and council asking us to vote on the Squamish Land Code. If we vote in favour of the land code, there will be drastic changes to all members' rights. We would like to point you to an article that was written by a lawyer named Janice Switlo, warning against land management codes. Ms Switlo acted as legal counsel for the Westbank Indian Band. She has worked for the Department of Justice and the Department of Indian Affairs. Based on her experiences, she is very concerned about the Land Code and the Framework Agreement on First Nation Land Management.
>
> Here is a summary of her concerns, and the implications for our people:
>
> The Land Codes are a "full scale assault on aboriginal beliefs — implementing the new regime results in the surrender of reserves and the abandonment of aboriginal title; they will remain 'reserves' but the underlying aboriginal title will be destroyed. This is a surrender to the Queen by

the Indian bands — once a land code is passed by referendum (ratified) a surrender to her majesty occurs.

"It's not a good day in Indian country for the band that adopts the new regime.

"It's a bad deal for aboriginal people who wish to preserve their rights and are misled by written words.

"The use of a verifier is to ensure there is no future prospect of being able to challenge what was entered into should the Indians figure out they were set up.

"The Framework Agreement destroys the original land rights; if the reserves are surrendered, proof of continuous ownership of the whole territory is forever lost.

"Janice Switlo's advice to First Nations considering a land code (such as the Squamish land code) for Indian bands scheduled to the First Nations Land Management Act is:

"Do not put a land code to a vote.

"The land code triggers everything.

"Its ratification causes the Framework Agreement to be automatically ratified as well.

"Band members may wish to consider legal action or going on record or otherwise paper trailing to challenge the federally held notion that chief and council can authorize the chief to sign such an agreement.

"Do not believe anyone who suggests, 'Oh well, let's just give it a try. What have you got to lose?'

"Actually – EVERYTHING.

"Given the concerns raised above, we are worried that the chief and council may not understand the full implications of the Squamish Land Code. Therefore, we ask the chief and council to carefully consider Janice Switlo's advice that Squamish Nation not put the land code to a vote. If chief and council decide to ignore the serious concerns raised by Janice Switlo, we ask all members to vote NO to the Squamish Land Code when the vote takes place on April 7–8, 2011.

"Respectfully submitted for your consideration."[16]

The two factions then set to work developing strategies to convince the membership that theirs was the right way to vote in the land code question. The band council began its campaign in February 2011with a bulletin sent to all band members; it included a section entitled "Why a Land Code? How was the Squamish Land Code developed?" and basic information on the code and the "Individual Agreement." However, the most interesting part of this bulletin was the timeline, which begins pre-1791 with first contact with Europeans and ends on April 9, 2013, when, if ratified by band members, the land code would come into force. The event listed for 1996 is the Squamish Nation's signing of the *Framework Agreement on Land Management*, while the land code only appears for the first time in 2003, after which date due diligence commenced, the reserve lands were surveyed, their environmental condition was reviewed and reported, and the first membership committee meetings were held to provide input into the code. The timeline also shows that eighteen of these meetings were held before lack of funding called a halt to them, but the committee was re-established in 2008 and held a further fourteen meetings before submitting a report to council in 2009. The following year the draft version of the code was written and reviewed by a membership committee, council and administrators (otherwise referred to as the "Land Code Working Group"), which made its own recommendations for further revisions. (The rules laid down in the Framework Agreement required that the code document had to be ready well before the ratification dates in order that band members had adequate time to read it, understand it, and ask questions.) According to this first bulletin from the council, band members had participated in the development of the land code in over forty meetings held since 2003, more than ninety members had been involved in committees and working groups, and there had been over six hundred "person meetings" invested by members. However, following the release of this bulletin, many band members asked, "If so many people were involved for so long, how come so few of us knew anything about any of this until now?"

Between February and April 2011 the band council raised a series of billboard advertisements on the reserves asking the members to vote "Yes" for the land code. They also continued to send out bulletins, each on a different aspect of the code. Bulletin 3 in March 2011, for example, focussed on housing and explained the "Housing Life Cycle" as it presently existed and the changes proposed in the code. At the beginning of March the council also distributed a "Voter Information Package," a spiral-bound book that included a copy of the 112-page *Squamish Land Code*, a 6-page executive summary of the code, a copy of the 24-page "Individual Agreement on First Nation Land Management between Squamish Nation and Her Majesty The Queen in Right of Canada," a 41-page draft of the Squamish Nation Community Ratification Process dated July 23, 2008, an executive summary of the *Framework Agreement* (5 pages), an executive summary of the *Land Management Act* (3 pages), a facsimile of the ballot, the question to be voted on, mail-in forms and identification papers and more — for a total of 182 pages.[17]

While this package was very thorough, it was also very technical, most of it written in legal and government terminology, so it was heavy reading for those not practised in translating such language into everyday English, and since Mazie was not the only person on the Squamish reserves who was unable to read, there were many who needed someone to explain what it was all about. Even for those who were literate, the terminology in the documents was daunting, and when the council belatedly realized this, they sent out a video to supplement the package. But adding to band members' frustration was the fact that they had barely four weeks to go through the material in the package and all the bulletins and to screen the video before the series of meetings the council had scheduled to provide an opportunity to ask questions. Between March 15 and March 25 there were six of these community meetings — two general meetings, two for elders and two for youth. Another two meetings were held in early April for families, and these included a meal.

At the end of March the council sent out a selection of the questions and answers that had been posed at the community meetings — they ranged from "What was going to be done regarding Native women and matrimonial real property?" to "What about the housing situation?" — but no definitive answers were provided because, it was explained, these problems would not be dealt with until *after* the land code was ratified. This did not sit well with the people as they wanted clear answers to the major questions they had asked. At this point, although there was no longer a shortage of information on the land code, the people lacked an understanding of its long-term implications, and they had just been told they would have to wait for answers until after the ratification of the land code. What, the people asked each other, were they actually voting for? What would these proposed changes mean for them, for their families — and for the Nation?

Mazie was very worried about what would happen to her certificates of possession under the new rules. When addressing the Senate committee, she had explained that they were her most valuable possessions; they gave her security because no one could take her land from her. However, Bill C-49 gave the band council the power to expropriate land for unidentified "community projects." The draft of the proposed land code did nothing to assuage her fears:

> My CPs would no longer exist. Instead, the land code says that all members with lots would have the same rights in the form of a Squamish Nation Residential Interest (SRI) — whatever that means. There won't be two sets of rules, one for CP holders like me and one for custom lot owners. I know my CPs were registered in the Indian Land Registry and were governed by *Indian Act* zoning bylaws and by the estate provisions of the *Indian Act*, section 48, and subject to the expropriation provisions of section 18(2). Wendy told me that. Under this land code they would be registered in the First Nations Land Registry and governed by the *Squamish Land Use Law*, the estate provisions of the *Indian Act* and subject to expropriation provisions of the proposed Squamish land code. I can say the words, but how do they expect us to understand all this bafflegab without time to have someone we trust explain it to us?

One thing was clear to Mazie, however: her fears were not groundless. Her CPs would be converted to SRIs and be under the jurisdiction of chiefs and councillors she did not trust, and they would have the power to expropriate her land.

Meanwhile, amid the flurry of council-sponsored meetings, bulletins and packages, Mazie and Jo-Ann were running a parallel campaign, sending out notices to explain why the people should vote against the code. Like the band council, they put up big boards asking the people to vote No and defeat the land code. Barred from using band-owned halls, Mazie held meetings in her home, Jo-Ann went on Facebook, chatted on line, contacted the media, both West Vancouver and North Vancouver city councils, and sent out emails to MLAs, the Governor General, the minister of Indian Affairs, Amnesty International, the United Nations, and, of course, the Queen. They gave out information to as many people as possible, explaining what the land code actually meant for members of the Nation.

Every day more and more people came to Mazie and Jo-Ann to ask questions; these were people who did not understand the documents sent to them by the council, and since they did not have enough time to read them before the community meetings, they didn't go. Some were surprised to learn that they had been named in the council bulletins as committee members; some recalled being asked various questions by councillors but had no recollection of actually sitting on any committees. At one of the general meetings some people stood up and denied that they were part of any committee; they had only signed in when they attended a community meeting.

Jo-Ann described what happened at the council information meeting that her family attended:

> At my family dinner they played the video and then asked for input through a paper questionnaire. The questions were mostly about what kind of housing did we want — condos? single family homes? or apartments? But we already knew that the housing list would not be affected by the land code; houses were not going to be built any faster and the list kept getting longer. So what was the point of asking? No one from chiefs and council even showed up to answer questions. Despite that, we had to sign in as proof that we had been involved [in the process].

Media interest in the outcome of the vote was intense, and concern rippled out to business leaders and the municipal councils of the Lower Mainland. Some civic leaders had heard that, if the land code was ratified, the Squamish Nation would build up to 12,000 condos on its Kitsilano and West Vancouver lands. The Lower Mainland Treaty Advisory Committee (LMTAC) issued a draft discussion paper on the possible impact for local municipalities. This paper estimated that 12,000 condos on Squamish land would result in almost 25,000 non-Aboriginals taking up residence on the reserves over the next twenty years; these people would not pay school taxes, property taxes, property transfer taxes or utility fees to either Metro Vancouver or Translink yet they would use schools and other facilities in those areas. Developers on Squamish lands would not have to deal with development charges that are used to cover the cost of parks and roads, and they wouldn't have to pay HST. The loss of revenue would be massive, and regular property owners would find themselves subsidizing those who had moved onto reserve lands. And what if other First Nations with desirable waterfront property — such as the Semiahmoo (White Rock) and Tsleil-Waututh (Burrard) — all decided to develop residential and business real estate? What about building codes, Work Safe and environmental issues? Paranoia was rampant.

By April 7 all the land code meetings had been held. The two factions had done what they could to influence the vote, and voting day had arrived. It was time for the people to speak. The polling stations were set up, and Mazie and Jo-Ann went down to vote and observe, and they noted that once again chiefs and council had decided to give out the disbursement cheques at the same time the vote was in progress. They decided to introduce themselves to the verifier and the person overseeing the vote, who asked Jo-Ann if she would like to be there when the ballots were being counted. She knew Jo-Ann was one of the "mistrusting ones" so her presence would help to demonstrate that the count was done properly. Jo-Ann agreed to be there and returned the following night with Mazie to watch as each ballot box was opened and the ballots counted. When the results were announced, it was clear that the people had spoken decisively. The results were:

2528   eligible voters

1367   ballots cast

547   Yes votes

808   No votes

12   spoiled ballots

The people of the Squamish Nation had defeated the land code.

"We won! We won!" Mazie, Jo-Ann and Wendy were ecstatic. All their hard work over the years had paid off. *The Framework Agreement* was null and void.

Word of the defeat spread rapidly. While the management of the Lower Mainland Treaty Advisory Committee, Metro Vancouver and Translink breathed a collective sigh of relief, the media was stunned by this turn of events. Native networks across the country, such as Turtle Island, and aboriginal newspapers and mainstream newspapers all asked the same question: Why did the Squamish people defeat the land code? Why did they turn down self-government?

The *Vancouver Sun*'s story on April 10 was typical of the media's reaction. The story, which was headlined "A Shocking Blow to Squamish Nation self-government efforts," expressed the general confusion:

> The Turtle Island Native Network reports that the rejection by Squamish Nation members of a proposed historic Land Code is, in fact, a rejection of self-government. By a vote of 808 to 547, the land management initiative, something the chief and council and their administrators have worked on for more than a dozen years, was soundly defeated.
>
> But why?
>
> All those many years of effort, expense and expectation, fell like a ton of bricks — when the voice and messages of the grassroots people resonated so loudly in the referendum results. In a world where First Nations ache for more control over their lives on the reserves,

comes this shocking statement from Squamish Nation elder and activist, 79-year-old Velma "Mazie" Baker: "The people don't want self-government."

In an interview with Turtle Island Native Network, Ms Baker explained that the majority of the Squamish people don't trust their elected officials and did not want to give them more power over their lives.

"They're not accountable — we don't know how much money there is or where it all goes." Mazie Baker says if you look around her community, you see the poverty, "people pushing buggies" (shopping carts?), a reference to the homeless and the ones barely surviving.

In a question aimed at both chief and council and Indian Affairs, she asks, "Who's looking after the Indians?" She explained that out of fear of things getting even worse, the people who rejected the Land Code would rather maintain the status quo of the Indian Act and Indian Affairs. Some day there might be community leadership they trust and that is accountable to the people, but she holds out little hope such a day will arrive.

In a theme familiar on reserves in many First Nations communities, Mazie Baker pointed to nepotism — the challenges created when one particular family has control of the community. "They get all the jobs," and benefits don't flow to people like her and others who delivered their powerful message as they voted against the Land Code.

Turtle Island Native Network also notes that Squamish Nation leaders immediately issued a letter to community members after the vote. In the letter, elected chief Gibby Jacob and council co-chairs Byron Joseph and Krisandra Jacobs, and band manager Glen Newman congratulated the membership on a "decisive and clear" vote "mandating that there will be no changes to the existing management of our Indian Reserve Lands

… We will not pursue the proposed Land Code without further consent of the membership. Our Nation will remain under the supervision of the Department of Indian and Northern Affairs for the management of our Indian Reserve Lands." The letter also included the promise that the leadership will seek community input on how to proceed now. "Chiefs and council look forward to hearing from membership about ways to improve the system of land management on our Indian reserves."

Squamish band member Wendy Lockhart Lundberg told Turtle Island Native Network what she believes led to the referendum results. "In my opinion, community members rejected the land code because of the manner in which it was implemented without consultation and without member mandate before the Framework Agreement was signed by Squamish Band Council in 1996. The FNLMA is piecemeal legislation that avoids significant treaty issues such as sovereignty and Aboriginal title. It is an authority delegated by the federal government and a significant departure from the treaty process that the Squamish people had entered into in good faith pursuant to the Openness Protocol signed by Canada, British Columbia and the Squamish Nation. The Openness Protocol clearly states that the Squamish people would mandate and ratify every step of the process. That did not happen with land codes under the FNLMA, and I think that the vote results evidence that the Squamish people would not accept that."[18]

In a story published in *The Chief* newspaper of Squamish on April 15 reporter David Burke wrote that:

In two days of voting last Thursday and Friday (April 7 and 8), members voted 808 to 547 against the Squamish Land Code, a measure put forward by the chiefs and council that would have seen local leaders gain authority over land use and environmental protection over the 849 hectares of on-reserve land on the North Shore, in Gibsons and in the Squamish area.

The turnout was just over half of the 2,528 eligible voters.

In the days leading up to vote, leaders had urged the measure's passage, saying they felt it offered the nation a chance to cast away at least a portion of the "paternal structure" imposed under the Indian Act. Some members, though, expressed concern about provisions in the land code surrounding expropriation of land and about the potential for authority to be concentrated in the hands of a few leaders. Xayiltenaat (Shirley Lewis), who led a small "no" demonstration outside Totem Hall on Thursday (April 7), said one problem is the document, written in legal language, was presented to the people only about a month before the vote. She added that, in general, she and others feel there hasn't been enough consultation with the membership on a variety of issues. "They have to answer to the people, but they're doing things on their own and we're not happy with it," she said.

Chief Ian Campbell on Tuesday (April 12) acknowledged that the timing issue was a big one raised by members. "The feedback that we've received so far has indicated that the membership didn't have enough time to really process the information about what would stem from the land code and because of that, they weren't prepared to endorse it," Campbell said.

A man who asked that he be identified by his hereditary name, Gausedis, said some who did read the document felt it left the door open to abuses by those in positions of authority. "There's no checks and balances and there's no protection from exploitation," he said while seated outside Totem Hall on Thursday.

Another man, who spoke on condition of anonymity, said, "I've read most of it and I've seen some good points, but I've also seen the door left open for some bad, bad decisions for our nation. There's too many holes in this document, and it's been pushed through too fast."

Gausedis said some don't feel the current chiefs and council adequately represent them and would like to see the nation go back to the hereditary representation system that existed before 1981.

"We want to see the hereditary system back in place — our laws, the way it used to be, with families looking after each other, not the people in power looking after their own," he said.

Said Campbell, one of four hereditary chiefs under the current system of representation, "The land code process has certainly triggered a lot of great dialogue among our membership. From that, there was a lot of discussion of issues surrounding our system, including land use and governance. If they'd like to change that [system], there's an opportunity to have that discussion and consider changing it."[19]

Mazie and her team had accomplished what many would have thought was impossible. But after this success, what was left for her to accomplish? She was now 79 years old — surely it was time to put up her feet and rest her creaky knees.

18

On April 12, 2011, Mazie Baker sat in a booth in the White Spot Restaurant at Park & Tilford Shopping Centre in North Vancouver, bouncing up and down with excitement over the defeat of the land code. She grinned at everyone and then announced, "I'm not done yet! We have 550 signatures on a petition to take to the general band meeting next week calling for a vote of no confidence in the chiefs and council."

Copies of the petition had been sent to the Canadian Human Rights Commission; the speaker of the Senate, the Honourable Noel A. Kinsella; the speaker of the House of Commons, the Honourable Andrew Scheer; the head office of the United Nations; the Vancouver office of Amnesty International; the minister of Aboriginal Affairs and Northern Development, the Governor General of Canada, Prime Minister Stephen Harper, and Her Majesty the Queen.

There was no stopping Mazie now. She was on a roll.

However, on April 17, the day of the meeting, Mazie told her niece Wendy Lockhart and Jo-Ann Nahanee, "I'm not gonna speak today because I'm not feeling very well. I wasn't gonna come, but you know there is no way I'm gonna miss this meeting." So she sat uncharacteristically silent in the meeting hall until the motion was presented, then just before the vote was called, she changed her mind, stood up and spoke the following words to her people:

> Hi, people. I just want to tell you, don't forget we almost got divided by those votes — 800 to 500 — and I want to tell you a little history about this '73 Act. Our old culture,

years ago, said, "Don't ever go under this '73 Act." And today it's the land codes. So it went from the '73 Act to Bill C-31 to Bill C-49, then it went under the *Land Management Act.* Now it's under land codes. So vote for what you have to vote for. Thank you.

She sat down and waited for the vote to be called. But it was not called that day because Mazie Baker suddenly collapsed against her niece. She had suffered a major heart attack and was rushed to Lions Gate Hospital. She died two days later on April 19, fighting for her people until the end.

On Thursday, April 21, and Friday, April 22, 2011, at the Chief Joe Mathias Centre on Capilano Road, Mazie Baker's life was honoured by members of the Squamish Nation (*Sḵwx̱wú7mesh Úxwumixw*), her loving and devastated family, and many, many others who had worked with her, fought with her, lost to her at cards, played bingo with her, paddled with her, laughed with her and loved her. On Thursday there was a viewing from 4:00 to 6:45 p.m., followed by a Catholic blessing and Shaker prayers at 7:00 p.m. Events the following day lasted all day, and the Centre was packed with her beloved people.

The family wore Montreal Canadian hockey jerseys in recognition of her passion for hockey and her favourite team. Keith Nahanee Jr. had created a video of photos and some of her favourite music. Jo-Ann Nahanee delivered a eulogy regarding Mazie's political battles for her people. Wendy Lockhart brought messages from Senator Pat Carney and other politicians and the many people Mazie had come into contact with across the country because, once people met Mazie, they never forgot her.

Her ceremony closed with some of the traditional songs of the pow-wow sung by Junior Waskewitch and the Squamish Nation Drummers and Singers (*tl'alhbi)* as everyone gathered to deliver their own words and prayers of respect.

Her coffin had been specially made with paddles as handles in honour of her love of paddling. She was carried by teams of pall bearers, all of whom who were proud to rest her on their shoulders during the procession to the longhouse. The street was lined with crowds of people paying homage, and the roads were closed by the police to allow her to pass without interruption on this, her last journey. The paddlers carried their painted paddles raised high. The drums beat and the voices soared as she was finally, gently, placed in the hearse to leave for the crematorium.

Following her departure, everyone returned to the Centre to share in the feast provided by the family. The rest of the evening was delivered in the Squamish language (*Sḵwx̱wú7mesh snichim*) with individual thanks given by the family to all who had helped Mazie on the day of her collapse in the council meeting. Many people, including elders, spoke and paid tribute to her, some in tears, some remaining strong in their loss. The committee members who had worked with her all wore pink t-shirts because it was her favourite colour and they promised to continue her fight. Mazie would have felt so loved and honoured by family and "her people," those she had spent most of her adult life fighting for and supporting in their times of need.

The Squamish Nation was in a state of shock. Their elder, their golden eagle who had listened, helped and fought for them, was gone. What was going to happen now? Was there anyone who could or would step into her shoes? Out of respect for her friend, Jo-Ann Nahanee asked Mazie's family if they would like her to continue with Mazie's work, and they told her that they would appreciate it as they knew that Mazie would want the work to continue. Jo-Ann, along with other members of the group who also wished to have the non-confidence vote completed, now formed a group that they called "Squamish Voices." When Mazie was stricken on April 17, Wilfred Baker, the chair of the meeting, had announced that the meeting would be adjourned until further notice. On April 20, 2011, the new group formally requested the chiefs and council to desist from engaging in any further business in connection with the land code as the people had spoken and they had said a resounding *No*. On May 2 a request was made to the council to reschedule the abruptly adjourned meeting and for the non-confidence vote to be completed, but the council delayed rescheduling it until September 9, 2012, when a special peoples' meeting was called and the vote was continued. Each councillor was named and the members voted on them individually using the wording of a motion from a peoples' meeting Mazie had called in 1985 to fire two councillors. (One had been fired, one had kept his job.) The motion and agenda combined both legal and customary or traditional form in order to cover all the bases. The motion read as follows:

> That the membership of the Squamish Indian Band agree with and recommend that (name of councillor) be dismissed from all his duties as an elected and non-elected band official or position and as an employee of the Squamish Indian Band.

Each in turn was voted out of office. Other motions had been added to the agenda regarding transparency in financial responsibilities, financial records, the removal of cheque-signing authority and the firing of several employees involved in the financial planning and activities of the band. The final motion was "that the membership of the Squamish Indian Band agree with and recommend that the *First Nations Commercial Industrial Development Act* be stopped, cease and desist as the Land Code had been voted down." Each of these motions also passed. The whole process took two and half hours because it had to be done twice in accordance with the band rule that motions from the membership had to be passed a second time. The group, therefore, held two consecutive meetings on the same day to meet that requirement, the first beginning at 2:00 p.m., the second at approximately 4:00 p.m.

The local media—the *North Shore News*, *The Chief*, and the *North Shore Outlook*—all carried articles with headings such as "Squamish Nation group 'fires' leadership," "Squamish Members call for Chief and Council to resign," and "Group aims to boot Squamish Council." But while it appeared to be a major sweep of the Squamish Nation's chiefs, council and administration officers, as they had on earlier occasions, those "booted out" refused to accept the will of the people. Chief Ian Campbell commented that the voting results were not legally binding and did not require the elected chiefs and council to step down. Nothing was going to happen until the next band elections in December 2013.

In March 2013, Parliament passed the *First Nations Financial Transparency Act*, which required that the 581 First Nations who are defined as Indian bands under the *Indian Act* must make their audited financial statements plus a schedule of remuneration and expenses of chief and council as well as the auditor's report on these documents available to their members as well as publish them on a website within 120 days of the end of each financial year. The purpose of the act was to enhance the financial accountability and transparency of First Nations by requiring public disclosure of finances and expenses, especially those related to the remuneration of elected members — in both their official and personal capacities. Punishment for not producing and publishing these statements was the withholding of federal funds.

The act addressed many of the issues that Mazie and her group had been challenging the chiefs and councillors over, and it allowed Jo-Ann Nahanee, Clarissa Antone and Bev Brown to legally demand answers to their questions about the Squamish Nation's finances. In fact, in October 2014 the RCMP opened an investigation into $1.5 million in missing Squamish Nation funds, and two council members were stripped of their duties although they were allowed to remain on council.[20]

However, in December 2015, Carolyn Bennett, minister of Indigenous and Northern Affairs in the new Liberal majority government, reinstated the funding retained under the *Transparency Act* and halted the compliance measures that had required bands to post detailed financial statements online. The minister also said that the government would suspend court actions against First Nations that had not complied with the terms of the act.

And so the battles continue … without Mazie Baker to lead the forces for good. But her example and her wonderful willpower and resourcefulness live on in the "Squamish Voices."

Acknowledgements

So many people from different spheres of my own life and Mazie's have been involved in the creation of this book, and all of them have added invaluable insights into Mazie's many-faceted life.

My special thanks go to:

Mazie herself, who taped so many hours of her story amid laughter, sadness, frustrations and successes. She will forever be the sister of my heart.

Mazie's children Gloria, Tammie, Tia, Roy (Bucky), Alf, Bert and Shawn, and grandchildren Keith Jr. (Bubbas), Riannon and Kanani, who spent so much time with me around the dining room table filling in the gaps and revealing their childhood memories. We laughed often and long.

Jackie Gonzalez and Jo-Ann Nahanee, members of the Skwxwú7mesh Úxwumixw (Squamish Nation), for providing support, documentations and Mazie stories and for sharing their personal insights.

Wendy Lockhart, whose years of fighting alongside Mazie, leading her through all the complex government documents, travelling the country with her to speak out for Native Women's rights are an example to all women.

Senator Pat Carney and Reform MP Ted White, both of whom supported Mazie in her political forays, for their generosity in providing written documents for her biography.

My thanks also go to:

North Vancouver Museum and Archives, especially Janet Turner, archivist; Sandra Boutilier, news research librarian at the Pacific Newspaper Group Library; Don Mcleod, vice-president, and his administrative assistant, Jocelyn Smith, of the Canada Fishing Company (Canfisco); Janice Switlo, lawyer, for her permission to use *Apple Cede*; Christopher Alcantara, associate professor at Wilfred Laurier University, for permission to use his paper on certificates of permission; Karrmen Krey, Stó:lō, a PhD student in the Cinema and Media Studies program at the University of California, Los Angeles, for permission to use her paper on enfranchisement. (I am proud to say that Karrmen is one of my former students at Thomas Haney Secondary in Maple Ridge, BC.)

Thank you to:

The Shuswap Association of Writers and The Shuswap Writers' Group for helping me through this whole long odyssey by listening to sections of the story and providing helpful critiques; Lynne Stonier Newman, Deanna Kawatski and Shirley DeKelver for your eagle eyes as you read the manuscript and spotted errors I had missed; Virginia McCausland who was so helpful in the creation of a new chapter one; Jacqueline Guest for endless assistance with my query letter and your friendship; Harold Rhenisch for agreeing to be my consultant for the overall manuscript. His advice and wisdom sharpened my focus and led me in some new directions; Vici Johnstone and the Caitlin Press team for believing that Mazie's story was worth telling, and Betty Keller for being an editor extraordinaire. And special thanks to Jo for your years of support and your patience, and for spending many hours in the basement translating the numerous audio tapes into transcripts.

Appendix

Original villages pre the 1923 Amalgamation

Eslha7án (Mission) I.R. No. 1

Ch'ích'elxwi7k̲w (Seymour) I.R. No. 2

Xwmélch'sten (Capilano) I.R. No. 5

Seṅák̲w (Kitsilano) I.R. No. 6

Skáwshen (Skowishun) I.R. No. 7

Ch'ék̲ch'ek̲ts (Chuckchuck) I.R. No. 8

P'uy̲áṁ (Poyam) I.R. No. 9

Skáwshen (Skowishin) I.R. No. 10

Ch'iyák̲mesh (Cheakmus) I.R. No. 11

Yekw'ts (Yookwits) I.R. No. 12

Puk̲wayúsm (Poquiosin) & S̲k̲emín (Skamain) I.R. No. 13

Wíwk̲'em (Waiwakum) I.R. No. 14

Íkwikws (Aikweks) I.R. No. 15

Siyí7ch'em (Seaichem) I.R. No. 16

Kewtín (Kowtain) I.R. No. 17

Yekw'ápsem (Yeakwapsem) I.R. No. 18 & I.R. No. 19

Mámxwem (Mamquam) I.R. No. 20

Squamish Island I.R. No. 21 (Expropriated)

Skwelwí7lem (Suiwailum) I.R. No. 22 (Expropriated)

(Ahtsam) I.R. No. 23 (Expropriated)

St'á7mes (Stawamus) I.R. No. 24

K̲'ík̲'elx̲en (Kailalahun) I.R. No. 25

Ch'ek̲w'élhp (Chekwelp) I.R. No. 26 I.R. No. 26a

(Chekwelp Schaltuuch) I.R. No. 27

Defense Island I.R. No. 28

KwumKwum I.R. No. 28a

Bibliography

Books

Birchwater, Sage. *Chiwid.* Vancouver: New Star Books, 1995.

Cardinal Harold. *The Unjust Society: The Tragedy of Canada's Indians.* Vancouver: M.G. Hurtig 1969; Douglas & McIntyre,1999.

Dunlop, Herbert Francis. *Andy Paull: As I knew Him and Understood His Times.* Vancouver: The Order of the O.M.I. (St. Paul's Province), 1989.

Gray Smith, Monique. *Tilly: A Story of Hope and Resilience.* Winlaw, BC: Sono Nis, 2013.

Mathews, Major J.S. *Conversations with Khahtsahlano 1932–1934.* Vancouver. 1955. Available online at Vancouver Archives.

Moran, Bridget. *Stoney Creek Woman: The Story of Mary John.* Vancouver: Arsenal Pulp Press, 1988.

Point Bolton, Rena and Richard Daly. *Xweliqwiya, The Life Story of a Stó:lō Matriarch.* Athabasca University Press, 2013.

Quintasket, Christine (pen name Mourning Dove). *Mourning Dove: A Salishan Autobiography.* Bison Books, 1994.

Reid, Martine J. and Daisy Sewid-Smith. *Paddling to Where I Stand: Agnes Alfred,* (Qwiqwasutinuxw noblewoman). Vancouver: UBC Press, 2004.

Robertson, Leslie, A. and the Kwagu'l Gixsan Clan. *Standing Up with Ga'axsta'las: Jane Constance Cook and the Politics of Memory, Church, and Custom.* Vancouver: UBC Press, 2012.

Sellars, Bev. *They Called Me Number One: Secrets of Survival at an Indian Residential School.* Talon Books, 2013.

Dictionary

Squamish Nation Education Department *Skwxwu7mesh Snichim-Xweliten Snichim Skexwts/Squamish-English Dictionary* University of Washington Press 2011

Newspapers

BC Raven's Eye

First Nations Drum

The Globe and Mail

Kahtou News

North Shore News

Squamish Chief

Vancouver Sun and *Province*

The National Post

Windspeaker

Museums and Archives

Canada Fishing Company-Canfisco http://www.canfisco.com/

North Vancouver Museum and Archives http://nvma.ca/

Internet

Museum of History and Industry (MOHAI) Seattle, Washington State http://www.mohai.org/

Vancouver Sun and *Province* Archives http://www.vancouversun.com/about-vancouver-sun/library.html

Squamish Nation http://www.squamish.net/about-us/

Vancouver Archives http://vancouverarchives.ca

http://www.vancouverarchives.ca/2012/07/27/conversations-with-khahtsahlano-is-available-online/

Articles and Papers

Alcantara, Christopher. PhD. *Individual Property Rights On Canadian Indian Reserves: The Historical Emergence and Jurisprudence of Certificates of Possession.* 2003 Political Science Faculty Publications. Paper 6.

Krey, Karrmen. *Enfranchisement.* http://indigenousfoundations.arts.ubc.ca/home/government-policy/the-indian-act/enfranchisement.html 2009 First Nations Study program UBC

Switlo, Janice G.A.E. B.Com. LLB. *Apple Cede: First Nations Land Management Regime. Canada's solution to decisively exterminate aboriginal title.* June 9, 1999. http://www.switlo.com/pdf/apple-cede.pdf

Government documents

The *Royal Proclamation of 1763*

The *Indian Act* 1876

Indian Act: Elections of Chiefs and Band Councils

http://laws-lois.justice.gc.ca/eng/acts/I-5/page-25.html#h-34

Indian Band Election Regulations. http://laws-lois.justice.gc.ca/eng/regulations/C.R.C.,_c._952/index.html

Amendments to the *Indian Act* 1876–1950. Revision of the *Indian Act* 1951

Amendments to the *Indian Act*, Bill C-31. 1985. http://www.parl.gc.ca/content/lop/researchpublications/bp410-e.htm

The First Nations Land Management Act (FNLMA). Bill C-49. 1999. http://laws-lois.justice.gc.ca/eng/acts/F-11.8/page-1.html

Framework Agreement section of Bill C-49. http://www.georgegordon-firstnation.com/documents/Executive-Summary-FA

First Nations Land Management Regime (option to develop land codes) part of Bill C-49. https://www.aadnc-aandc.gc.ca/eng/1327090675492/1327090738973

Bill C-7: *The First Nations Governance Act.* 2002 (Not Passed) http://publications.gc.ca/Collection-R/LoPBdP/LS/372/372c7-e.htm

Endnotes

1. Proceedings of the Standing Senate Committee on Aboriginal People, Issue 28 — Evidence, May 4, 1999 (afternoon sitting). Page 1.

2. Ibid.

3. Proceedings. Page 2.

4. Ibid.

5. Ibid.

6. *Vancouver Province*, April 25, 1999. Page A29.

7. Ibid.

8. Proceedings of the Standing Senate Committee on Aboriginal People, Issue 28 — Evidence, May 4, 1999 (afternoon sitting). Page 2–3.

9. Ibid. Page 3–4.

10. Ibid. Page 4.

11. Ibid. page 7.

12. Ibid.

13. Ibid. Page 5.

14. Maheu, Hon. Shirley and Hon. Eileen Rossiter, *A Hard Bed to Lie in: Matrimonial Property on Reserve*. Report of the Standing Senate Committee on Human Rights. 37th Parliament, 2nd Session, 8th Report. 2003. Page 1–2.

15. Switlo, Janice G.A.E. *Apple Cede: First Nations Land Management Regime*. Tako Tomes. June 9, 1999. With permission.

16. Document supplied by Jo-Ann Nahanee and used with permission.

17. Jo-Ann Nahanee provided her copy of the package and gave permission for it to be used as a reference.

18. *Vancouver Sun*, April 10, 2011.

19. Glacier Media Inc. Licensed by *Squamish Chief* for republication in the *Biography of Mazie Baker, Squamish Nation Elder*.

20. http://www.piquenewsmagazine.com/whistler/rcmp-opens-file-in-to-missing-squamish-nation-cash/Content?oid=2570967